RØDKÅL

CAFÉ LONDON

BRUNCH, LUNCH, COFFEE AND AFTERNOON TEA

EDITED BY ZENA ALKAYAT

REVIEWS BY NICKY EVANS, PIPPA BAILEY, ANDY HILL AND NICOLA TRUP

PHOTOGRAPHS BY KIM LIGHTBODY

F

FRANCES
LINCOLN

KITCHEN

CONTENTS

INTRODUCTION

London is home to brilliantly brewed coffee, unparalleled cake stands and perfect cups of tea - you just have to know where to find them. And that's where this guidebook comes in.

From hundreds of cafés, coffee shops and afternoon tea destinations across the city, Café London sorts the spectacular from the merely mediocre by handpicking 100 of the very best places to pull up a chair and take respite.

Chapters cover all of your café needs, helping you find the best brunches to kick start your weekend, lovely lunches to enjoy with friends, the silkiest lattes to lounge over, and the fluffiest cakes and fanciest afternoon teas to indulge in. At the end of each chapter, you'll also find 'seven more' extra special places that just had to be squeezed in.

So whether you're after a simple brunch in a neighbourhood hangout, or a glamorous afternoon in the company of some loose-leaf tea and fondant fancies, this insider's guide is your essential companion.

This New York export has become a favourite among Londoners, and cafés across the capital are scrambling to meet demand. The following eateries are the cream of the crop for indulgent late breakfasts.

BRUNCH

ZOFFANY
PAINTS

LOWRY & BAKER

A visit to the cosy (some may say slightly cramped) Lowry & Baker is a bit like having brunch in someone's ramshackle kitchen. The narrow space is crammed with borderline-rickety furniture – sometimes sent wobbling by the jostles of staff members, brunchers and people milling by the door waiting keenly for a table – and features a counter topped with brilliant cakes and bakes. It's homey, cute and very popular with Notting Hill locals, particularly at the weekends, when the kitchen dishes out an excellent brunch menu. The typical brunch elements are served in classic combinations – smoked salmon, avocado, eggs – and the coffee is Monmouth. If you're making a day of it among Golborne Road's market stalls and shops, this is a lovely little retreat.

—

339 Portobello Road, W10 5SA.
No phone.
www.lowryandbaker.com
Ladbroke Grove tube.

CARAVAN

The food paradise of Exmouth Market – a pedestrianised street brimming with restaurants (and sometimes food stalls) – has seen many businesses come and go over the years, but Caravan has remained a successful constant. The dining room, with its careworn tables, bistro chairs, eclectic prints and bare bulbs, looks the part in this cool but chic part of town, and it occupies a prime street-corner spot with windows overlooking the market (bag a bench outside to get closer to the action). Tuck into an all-day menu of inspired east-meets-west sharing plates, such as fragrant spiced quail with tahini-laced yoghurt and vibrant chickpea salad – they make for perfect brunches and laid-back, lazy lunches alongside more classic sourdough/egg options. Don't leave without ordering a top-notch espresso, made with a blend of beans roasted on site – or try one of the regularly changing filter coffees.

—

11-13 Exmouth Market, EC1R 4QD.

020 7833 8115

www.caravanonexmouth.com

Farringdon tube.

BRANCHES: King's Cross N1C 4AA.

TINA, WE SALUTE YOU

This tiny corner café in Dalston has a devoted local fanbase, no doubt drawn in by the small but perfectly formed menu of essentials. There's excellent coffee by Alchemy, a couple of tempting homemade cakes and a short brunch menu starring offerings such as a stack of fluffy pancakes, brioche French toast, and poached eggs with avocado. A convivial communal table topped with condiments from Marmite to Nutella makes the tight squeeze bearable, but if you want to stretch your legs there's a larger branch by the Olympic Park: this one has space for a more comprehensive all-day menu, as well as beer and cocktails, and is brilliantly located alongside green lawns and a children's play area. Both cafés make a fuss over Tina – not the owner, but rather the subject of a kitsch 1960s painting by JH Lynch.

—

47 King Henry's Walk, N1 4NH.
020 3119 0047
www.tinawesaluteyou.com
Dalston Kingsland Overground.
BRANCHES: East Village E20 1FT.

LANTANA

Hidden down a boutique-lined alley off hectic Goodge Street, Lantana is usually filled with the area's arty types. The close-set tables and high perches aren't everyone's cup of tea – you won't find mummies with buggies or all-business executives here – but for informal meet-ups, Lantana's brand of casual all-day Antipodean-style brunches are just right. On the menu, towering breakfast burgers filled with sausage, bacon, egg, smoked cheddar and spinach vie for attention with the likes of poached egg and smashed avocado on sourdough, or French toast with banana and pecans. The drinks list is all about the Alchemy coffee, with a few wines and beers too. Larger groups should head to the communal table downstairs – but if you can't get a seat, there's a Lantana takeaway next door.

—

13 Charlotte Place, W1T 1SN.
020 7637 3347
www.lantanacafe.co.uk
Goodge Street tube.
BRANCHES: Camden NW1 8AF; Shoreditch EC1Y 1HQ.

SUNDAY

Was there ever a better name for a brunch spot than Sunday? It's one that speaks of poring over the paper with friends as late morning turns into a sleepy afternoon. You may not be able to stay quite that long at this shabby-chic café-restaurant in Barnsbury, as competition for tables is fierce, but you won't be rushed. It's open for dinner three nights a week, but brunch (served daily except Monday) is the speciality, and you've a creative menu to choose from. Try the delicious corn fritters with smoked salmon and avocado, or the cornbread waffle with pork belly, pit beans and fried eggs. If you're feeling extra indulgent, you can round things off with a crisp, buttery croissant or gooey slice of toasted banana bread. It is Sunday, after all.

—

169 Hemingford Road, N1 1DA.
020 7607 3868
www.facebook.com/sundaybarnsbury
Caledonian Road & Barnsbury Overground.

TRADE

Trade is a very zen place to chill out over a long lazy brunch with its mellow décor and blooming, flower-pot-laden terrace. Lucky, since you'll want to linger over your brunch. There's a big menu, from simple scrambled eggs on toast with a side of chorizo to a pile of Trade's own pastrami (made in the café's backyard smokery), which is elaborately served with a toasted cholla roll and poached eggs, and comes glistening with hollandaise. The handmade philosophy stays through into lunch, with more house-smoked deli meats in generous sandwiches, as well as grilled cheese on artisan sourdough. There's homemade cakes, coffee from small-batch roasters and fine teas. There's really nothing more to ask for.

—

47 Commercial Street, E1 6BD.
020 3490 1880
www.trade-made.co.uk
Aldgate East tube.

E PELLICCI

If you crave a solid, hangover-quashing fry-up with a generous side-order of banter, this Grade II-listed Bethnal Green institution (and former haunt of the notorious Kray twins) is the best in town. The handsome, wood-panelled interior (reverently adorned with signed shots of cockney icons Kat Slater and Grant Mitchell) makes a cushty spot to peruse the back pages over an egg sandwich washed down with builders' tea. What really makes this caff a destination, though, is the warm welcome from Nev, scion of the Italian clan that first set up shop here in 1900. A genuine 'character', nothing escapes a big-hearted mickey-take from this East End geezer, be it the weather, your daft haircut or the football scores (heads up – he's a Spurs man).

—

332 Bethnal Green Road, E2 0AG.
020 7739 4873
Bethnal Green tube.

ESTERS

Just far enough off the beaten Stokey track that you'll likely get a table at any time of day, this tiny backstreet gem is a cracking place to grab a bite. Yes, the yummy mummies have colonised it, but only because it's really, really good; we defy you to find a more tantalisingly billed brunch than French toast with roasted strawberries, caramelised white chocolate, rosewater and crème fraîche. The menu has a connoisseur's depth, all the way through to the pastries (which include kouign-amaan, a Brittany speciality) and the impressive array of long-leaf teas. If you crave a caffeine spike, the latte is as smooth and velvety as the best in London. Special mention to the décor – Esters totally rocks a spry, Danish look, all smart-brushed concrete and metal, with a pretty garden out the back.

—

55 Kynaston Road, N16 0EB.
020 7254 0253
www.estersn16.com
Stoke Newington Overground.

the Counter

COUNTER CAFÉ

This local institution doesn't just serve coffee, it roasts its own – so you can buy bags of the stuff to take home after you've enjoyed a delicious cup. In true Hackney Wick style, Counter Café is housed in a converted warehouse (neighbouring a gallery and gift shop), and at weekends it's packed with a local trendy crowd. But brave the queue (or get up early) and you'll be rewarded with an eclectic choice of breakfasts. Like eggs? There's plenty, from Benedict to Turkish. Plus more unusual contenders, such as the incredible radish and apple coleslaw alongside potatoes, bacon, eggs and chickpeas. Counter is right on the canal, across from the Olympic Park, so hustle for a table with waterside views, or if the weather's playing nice then sit out on the café's pontoon and watch the boats drift past.

—

7 Roach Road, E3 2PA.
No phone.
www.counterproductive.co.uk
Hackney Wick Overground.

STORIES

If you've been to east London bar-venues The Book Club and The Queen of Hoxton, you won't be surprised to learn this Broadway Market café-bar is their younger sibling. In fact, it looks like the missing link between the two – it's inherited TBC's bare brick walls and laid-back vibe, combining it with the Queen's bright colours and hanging plants. With all-day brunch and mean bloody Marys, Stories is practically designed for hangovers. Big hearty full-English style breakfasts (with refined twists, such as red pepper and chilli ketchup, or the odd brioche bun) sit alongside granola or buttermilk pancakes. If you're too late for brunch (which finishes at 4pm), the lunchtime burger menu is brilliant (the beef and chorizo is not to be missed), or stick around for a selection of bar food later in the day (think pulled pork nachos with a side of polenta chips).

30-32 Broadway Market, E8 4QJ.
020 7254 6898
www.storiesonbroadway.com
Homerton or London Fields Overground.

HACKNEY BUREAU

If you're taking a lazy stroll along the Regent's Canal, veer off at Hackney's Mare Street, where you'll find this café-bar-restaurant on a slightly scruffy, graffiti-clad corner. Having started out as a gallery in 2010, Hackney Bureau later added a kitchen and now serves breakfast, lunch and dinner, but stays true to its roots with rotating exhibitions. Brunch includes egg and avocado-based combos and bowls of tasty bircher muesli, plus there's a changing menu of more inventive and substantial lunch and dinner dishes. The bar serves craft beers and cocktails, or you can keep it teetotal the fun way with a Caravan coffee. Pick an outdoor table or a window seat for optimum people-watching, particularly on Saturdays when Londoners stream past on their way to Broadway Market, just around the corner.

—

3 Mare Street, E8 4RP.
020 8533 6083
www.hackneybureau.com
Cambridge Heath Overground.

CREAM

This spacious, low-key café on a quiet London back street is classic Shoreditch: kitted out with industrial-chic fittings and statement lighting; and filled with Lululemon-clad yoga devotees and freelancers busy working on laptops. The brunch menu is a strength, ranging from light bites such as homemade granola, to blow-out options such as airy scrambled eggs topped with thick slices of cold-smoked salmon or a whole ball of creamy burrata with spicy, smoky chorizo and roasted peppers. The Campbell & Syme coffee is good – and all the better paired with something fresh from the wooden counter, such as a thick-filled sandwich wrapped in wax paper, or a slice of delicious three-tiered carrot cake.

—

31 New Inn Yard, EC2A 3EY.
020 7247 3999
www.cream-shoreditch.com
Shoreditch High Street Overground.

GINGER & WHITE

This bijou café just off Hampstead High Street is the perfect place to read the Sunday papers over brunch – if you can get a spot at the large communal table, that is. Once you're in, the compact size works in its favour as everyone piles in, creating a relaxed, friendly feel. Kids – more than welcome – will enjoy Marmite soldiers and soft boiled eggs, while adults will be torn between homemade baked beans with chorizo and comfortingingly childish fish finger sandwiches. The Square Mile coffee is excellent (flat whites, ristrettos and cortados all well-executed) and the choice of enticing cakes on the counter is almost too much – opt for an apple crumble muffin, which is just the breakfast side of sweet.

—

4a-5a Perrins Court, NW3 1QS.
020 7431 9098
www.gingerandwhite.com
Hampstead tube.
BRANCHES: Belsize Park NW3 4TG.

SEVEN MORE

- **KOPAPA**
  Unbeatabe weekend brunches in Covent Garden courtesy of Kiwi chef Peter Gordon: expect big, exciting flavours.
  32-34 Monmouth St, WC2H 9HA. Leicester Square tube.

- **NO 11 PIMLICO ROAD**
  Once a pub, this Chelsea spot is bright, slick and attractive – perfect for mums-who-brunch.
  11 Pimlico Rd, SW1W 8NB. Sloane Square tube.

- **GASTRO**
  This bistro could have been lifted directly from Montmartre: dig into excellent eggs atlantique and steak au frites.
  67 Venn St, SW4 0BD. Clapham Common tube.

- **SAWYER & GRAY**
  Cosy and homely Islington café with ambitious spirit and a love of good ingredients. Don't miss the filter coffee.
  290 St Paul's Rd, N1 2LH. Highbury & Islington tube.

- **ROCHELLE CANTEEN (pictured)**
  Weekday breakfast only, spartan choice (granola; eggs on toast), but worth it to brunch in a converted school bike shed.
  Arnold Circus, E2 7ES. Shoreditch High Street Overground

- **HASH E8**
  A dedicated brunch bar: you'll get eggs all-week long, and pancakes, hash and French toast for breakfast, lunch and dinner.
  170 Dalston Lane, E8 1NG. Hackney Downs Overground.

- **THE BREAKFAST CLUB**
  All day brunch in the retro-themed surrounds of this ever-popular (queues likely) breakfast-dedicated caff.
  Seven branches, including 11 Southwark Street, SE1 1RQ. London Bridge tube.

An informal café lunch can be a glorious thing, and there are destinations across London that think that the midday meal deserves far better than a soggy cheese sandwich. The cafés in this chapter elevate the humble lunch to something truly special.

LUNCH

KIPFERL

Billed as an Austrian coffeehouse, Kipferl wears its theme lightly. It's slick and contemporary, and would feel almost Scandinavian were it not for a counter teeming with sachertorte, apfelstrudel and guglhupf (that's a marbled budt cake). Almost all of the ingredients, including beer and wine, are sourced from Austria, which means you can order a delightfully evocative skiing-holiday spread of wurst, sauerkraut and mountain cheeses. House specialities are beef gulyas (goulash) with homemade egg noodles, and the veal schnitzel, served with a sharp, pickled salad. For breakfast, there's bauernfruehstueck (fried eggs, bacon and potatoes), or if you're looking to trim down for the slopes, a 'Sporty Breakfast' of granola, yoghurt, fruit and mint. Coffee is lovely, and served Austrian-style with a glass of water and a little chocolate on the side: *wunderbar.*

—

20 Camden Passage, N1 8ED.
020 7704 1555
www.kipferl.co.uk
Angel tube.
BRANCHES: Ladbroke Grove W10 5NL.

✳ THE LONDON PARTICULAR

Bringing rigorous seasonality and gentrified flavours (lime aioli, celeraic fritters) to the discerning denizens of SE14, this tidy little spot beside New Cross Overground station is worthy of being a destination café. Lunch is the star, as the kitchen is ambitious, creative and talented. The café also does a fine daily breakfast (the sausage sandwich with 'shallot relish' is divine), as well as simple cake and coffee (beans sourced from HR Higgins of Mayfair, offering a more Italianate grind than the Aussie blends which are so popular across London). On weekend evenings, fancier fare comes to the fore, though served on informal sharing plates, in keeping with the rough-hewn, intimate vibe of the room. Craft beer and decent wines are on offer, and next door the same crew run 'LP Bar', a triumphantly crazy, airliner-themed cocktail bar.

—

399 New Cross Road, SE14 6LA.
020 8692 6149
www.thelondonparticular.co.uk
New Cross Overground.

✷ OTTOLENGHI

Yotam Ottolenghi's mini-empire of deli-bakeries has spawned many copycats, but its window displays of billowing, pastel-coloured meringues and wonderful cakes and tarts triumphs as the most tempting. Although sweet treats may be the honey trap, Ottolenghi made his name with fresh, vegetable-heavy dishes that fuse Middle Eastern and Mediterranean cuisines and zingy, unusual flavours: think manouri and za'atar breakfast frittata sprinkled with sumac; a lunchtime salad of caramelised sweet potatoes with burnt-aubergine yoghurt, basil and toasted seeds; and dinner options that include miso-glazed mackerel with green mango and carrot pickle. The à la carte is pricey, but lunch is great value given the quality of ingredients and care taken in the kitchen. Ottolenghi is rightly popular throughout the day, so expect to wait for a table.

—

287 Upper Street, N1 2TZ.
020 7288 1454
www.ottolenghi.co.uk
Angel or Highbury & Islington tube.
BRANCHES: Belgravia SW1X 8LB; Notting Hill W11 2AD; Spitalfields E1 7LJ.

✷ ALBION

It may call itself a 'caff' but Albion is far from a greasy spoon. Co-owned by design legend Terence Conran, it's got a simple, classic aesthetic – none of the usual Shoreditch jumble-sale look here – and doubles up as a high-end deli and bakery (there's also a bar and rooftop restaurant above). Beyond the bottles of posh lemonade, baskets of fruit and crisp baguettes, the café serves hearty breakfasts (fried duck eggs on toast, for example) and a comprehensive all-day menu of British classics, ranging from roast chicken sandwiches via salt beef and split green pea broth to a game pie big enough for two to share. Grab youself a kerbside alfresco seat and watch the Shoreditch rabble go by.

—

2-4 Boundary Street, E2 7DD.
020 7729 1051
www.albioncaff.co.uk
Shoreditch High Street Overground.
BRANCHES: Redchurch Street E2 7DJ; Bankside SE1 9FU.

✷ BRIXTON VILLAGE

Thanks to some innovative thinking, Brixton Village – once a neglected, half-empty market – has transformed into a thriving hub for start-up businesses, and is now a bona fide destination for both tourists and Londoners. There are so many delicious things on offer on every row of the indoor market that the best option is a food crawl. Start with a freshly made waffle from Mediterranean café Wild Caper (pictured above) or try one of its luxurious brunches made with Clarence Court eggs. Next, take time out with a flat white at Antipodean pitstop Federation Coffee (and, if you have space, a delicious raspberry friand). After a little shopping and market browsing, you might find belly space for a Middle Eastern-style wrap stuffed with, say, chargrilled halloumi and spicy Merguez sausage, from former supperclub French & Grace. It's all fabulous budget food, so expect crowds, a bit of hustle and lots of atmosphere.

—

Brixton Village, SW9 8LB.
Wild Caper: 11a-13 Market Row, 0207 737 4410.
Federation Coffee: Unit 77-78, no phone.
French & Grace: Unit 19, 020 7274 2816.
www.brixtonmarket.net/brixton-village
Brixton tube.

EXPRESS FUNDS
27/28

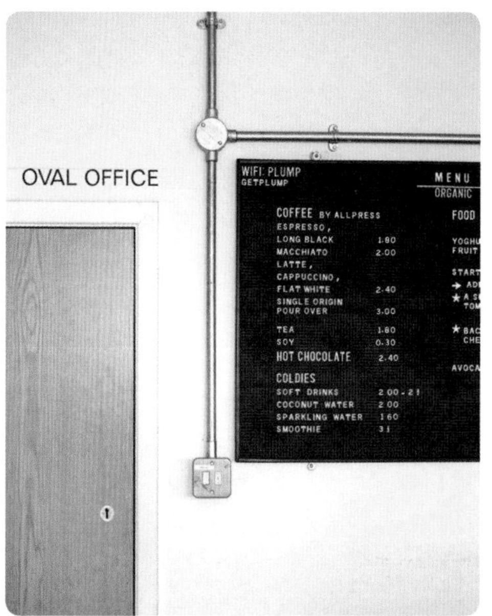

✺ PLUMP

Navigate the sullen East End wasteland that incongruously surrounds Plump (unfinished industrial units, rusty gas holders, graffitied stretch of canal), and you're in for a proper treat. Grab a window-facing stool if you yearn to just ponder the stark concrete outside; or pull up a seat at the giant communal table for a more convivial time. Plump is something of a sanctuary, with homely cakes, kindly staff and a really good pour over coffee. The menu changes with what's in season (check its Instagram @plumpcafe for a reliable daily heads-up), though you can expect the likes of stuffed red peppers, broccoli, bean and quinoa salad, and fat falafel and pesto sarnies. For breakfast, tuck into the usual classics including soft boiled eggs and soldiers, and a chilli and avocado toast that's hard to beat.

—

11 The Oval, E2 9DU.
020 3137 2243
www.plumpcafe.com
Cambridge Heath Overground.

✷ FOXCROFT & GINGER

Spread over two floors on one of the few streets that still retains some of Soho's original gritty charm, Foxcroft & Ginger doesn't just do hot food and sandwiches – it does slow-braised beef stew with pancetta crumble, and a coconut chicken laksa sandwich. And all at wallet-friendly prices. It also lays claim to one of the best breakfasts in town: the poached eggs, pedantically but perfectly poached at 63°C for an hour, are spot-on. You'll find them served with roasted mushrooms and truffled hollandaise on sourdough, or in the eggs Benedict alongside tasty pulled duck. For something lighter, the Chelsea buns are delightfully sticky, and you can also get your hands on a cruffin (yes, part croissant, part sourdough, part muffin).

—

3 Berwick Street, W1F 0DR.
No phone.
www.foxcroftandginger.co.uk
Oxford Circus tube.
BRANCHES: Dalston (at Beyond Retro) N16 7XB; Stepney Green E1 4TT.

Snackistan
Extras~
for Squiddlywinks:
Junior Meze platter -
~houmous, falafel, olives,
pitta Nothing too scary
£2-75
& if they eat all of that
-ice cream fruit + naughty
bits £2-50

✷ PERSEPOLIS

Despite myriad grocery distractions packed onto shelves in this unique, treasure-trove Persian deli-cum-café, you'll always spot owner Sally Butcher thanks to her red hair and cheerful greeting. She and her jovial Iranian husband run this Peckham peculiarity with an intoxicating mix of passion, humour and energy – their drive evidenced by the pages from Sally's many cookbooks, which decorate the walls. Everything on the menu is vegetarian – and refreshingly cheap. Order a generous mezze platter, eggs scrambled with a swirl of harissa, or the hotpot of the day. The only meats are sweetmeats: try the honey-doused baklava, or the spectacular saffron-laced banana split topped with pistachios, rosewater syrup and boozy cherries. Then browse the store to recreate the experience at home.

28-30 Peckham High Street, SE15 5DT.
020 7639 8007
www.foratasteofpersia.co.uk
Peckham Rye Overground.

GRANGER & CO

Anyone expecting Aussie chef Bill Granger's London restaurant to be as scrappily informal as his TV persona will be surprised: this smart, bustling brasserie occupying a high-ceilinged corner site on Westbourne Grove is all sky-high mirrors, giant blooms and gilt edging, with on-the-ball staff and a well-to-do clientele to reflect its money-washed location. This is Bill in business mode; you, however, can sit back and take it easy. Enticing brunch and lunch dishes demonstrate why Granger first captured our culinary imagination – try the crispy courgette fritters with creamy tahini dip, grilled halloumi, and a fresh, citrus-dressed salad, or make like a local and sip a flute of champagne at the swanky room-length bar. Free side order of celeb-spotting with every visit.

—

175 Westbourne Grove, W11 2SB.

020 7229 9111

www.grangerandco.com

Westbourne Park or Notting Hill tube.

BRANCHES: Clerkenwell EC1R 0HA; King's Cross N1C 4AG.

✵ FLEET RIVER BAKERY

With more chains than a 90s hip-hop video, Holborn can lack soul. But indie beacon Fleet River Bakery (named after the 'lost river' that courses beneath central London from Hampstead to the Thames), gives the place a much-needed neighbourhood feel. Patronised by the legal eagles of nearby Lincoln's Inn Fields (as well as some savvy tourists), on weekday lunchtimes the queue regularly snakes out of the door. And with good reason: delicious quiches and seasonal salads (fennel, orange and dill for instance) are carefully made, and the yummy frittata is something of a local legend. Naturally, bakery goods are key (the clue is in the name) – hazelnut millionaire shortbread, lemon ripple crunch cake and amazing scones are all baked in the kitchen downstairs.

—

71 Lincoln's Inn Fields, WC2A 3JF.
020 7691 1457
www.fleetriverbakery.com
Holborn tube.
BRANCHES: Fleet Kitchen, Bloomsbury WC1H 0JW.

✷ THE SPOKE

The Spoke is a friendly neighbourhood joint housed in a spruced-up pub, serving a morning-to-evening menu and frequented mostly by locals. Inside, the repurposed space is high-ceilinged and light, with beautiful wooden floors, a grey-tiled bar and industrial shelving behind. The brunch menu is tasty (porridge; French toast; a great full English), and the coffee smooth. But the much-billed burgers are the highlight (mature beef and cheese; prawn po'boy; and 'Japanese' mayo), which you can order alongside a swift lunchtime half. Though Spoke is marketed as a bike-friendly café (there is little reference to this cycling theme besides the name), during the week you'll mostly find it littered with four wheels (pushchairs) and local mums, while weekends attract a slightly younger and notably more bearded crowd, perhaps with a bike in tow.

—

710 Holloway Road, N19 3NH.
020 7263 4445
www.thespokelondon.com
Archway tube or Upper Holloway Overground.

✹ FERNANDEZ & WELLS

This laid-back Antipodean-style café plays host to a steady stream of Soho's discerning workers throughout the day – particularly creative types impressing their clients, or lunching with colleagues. The attraction is threefold: good-quality coffee (a single-origin Has Bean blend); lunch ranging from ciabatta filled with deli favourites to savoury toasted croissants; plus cakes that mean business by sourdough bakery Blue Door (try the buttery, sugar-coated Eccles cakes or prettily drizzled lemon crunch loaf). Each outpost of Fernandez & Wells (there are six in total, all varying in size) does its own thing – around the corner on Lexington Street, the original branch serves excellent tapas and wine late into the evening – but all share a rough-and-ready urban aesthetic that shows a great eye for design.

—

73 Beak Street, W1F 9SR.
0207 287 8124
www.fernandezandwells.com
Piccadilly Circus tube.
BRANCHES: Tottenham Court Road WC2H 8LP; Duke Street W1K 5NR; Lexington Street W1F 9AL; Aldwych (at Somerset House) WC2R 1LA (see p131); Exhibition Road SW7 2HF.

✷ FINK'S SALT & SWEET

This super-friendly neighbourhood deli-café opened in a former butcher's shop on a quiet Finsbury Park side street. There's a Scandi-style minimalism to its outfitting (school chairs, white tiles, lots of grey), as well as its menu, which features a salmon board and laid-back mix of charcuterie, cheeseboards and sandwiches (avocado, harissa and goat's cheese is a good choice). Coffee is excellent, cakes are fresh and delicious and the service is stellar. The shelves are also stacked with lovely deli items to buy and take home, from posh biscuits to unusual spreads. In the evening, Fink's operates as a cosy dinner den with unusual small plates and a strong wine list. If you're in the area (the Sylvanian Families shop is a few doors down, together with a brilliant bike shop and antiques shop), Fink's is very hard to resist.

—

70 Mountgrove Road, N5 2LT.
No phone.
www.finks.co.uk
Finsbury Park or Arsenal tube.

EVENING MENU
SMALL PLATES
SQUARE ROOT SODA
HANDMADE IN HACKNEY
GINGER BEER, LEMONADE, RHUBARB,
CITRUS CRUSH (BLOOD ORANGE), APPLE
CASCARA CLUB
SUFFOLK COLDPRESS APPLE JUICE 1·8
FRESHLY SQUEEZED ORANGE JUICE 1·8
SPARKLING WATER 1·5 / 3·5
COKE / DC 1·2
BEERS: MEANTIME LONDON LAGER 3·4
PARADISE PALE ALE 3·7
GOSNELL'S MEAD 4
JACK OF CLUBS 3·8

✷ DAYLESFORD ORGANIC

In a city teeming with restaurants that pay lip service to ethical, sustainable and organic practices, Daylesford Organic stands out as the real deal. Most of the artfully presented meat, soil-flecked vegetables and artisan cheeses in its chi-chi ground-floor shop come from its pioneering Gloucestershire-based farm, and everything else is organic and sustainable – although you may have to remortgage your house to shop here. The mezzanine café-restaurant, whose walls are inset with huge cross-sections of tree trunk, reinforces the brand's nature-first philosophy. Dishes such as caper- and herb-strewn smoked salmon on pumpernickel bread, topped with a golden-yolked hard-boiled egg, are popular with well-heeled regulars. Don't miss the bakes, either: Daylesford's light, golden-crusted scones with delectable clotted cream and berry-packed jam are a delicious advert for organic living.

—

208-212 Westbourne Grove, W11 2RH.
020 7313 8050
www.daylesford.com
Ladbroke Grove tube.
BRANCHES: Pimlico SW1W 8LP; Marylebone W1U 4AU; Mayfair (at Selfridges) W1A 1AB.

✹ J+A CAFÉ

The first pleasing thing about this café is its location: finding the right alley off the roaring Clerkenwell Road and spying the cheery string lighting is like unearthing a small treasure. Housed in a former diamond-cutting factory, J+A is split into thirds – there's a ground-floor café with open-plan kitchen; more tranquil seating upstairs; and across the yard, a bar. They all share the same brilliantly stripped-back but warm aesthetic, and they're all looked after by Johanna and Aoife Ledwidge. The sisters are keen on sourcing good ingredients (proper craft beers in the bar, proper tea in the café), as well as wholesome comfort food (pies, stews, soda bread) and remembering their Irish roots – you'll get Tayo crisps on the side of your steak sandwich and the chocolate Guinness cake isn't to be missed.

—

1-4 Sutton Lane, EC1M 5PU.
020 7940 2992
www.jandacafe.com
Farringdon tube.

SNAPS + RYE
SNAPS RYE
DANISH EATERY & TAKEAWAY
SNAPS + RYE
DANISH TASTINESS
DELIVERY
020 8964 3004
BULLITT

✷ SNAPS + RYE

Found on a stretch of Golborne Road that still has some of that rickety, run-down charm that Notting Hill has sadly lost, Snaps + Rye brings a welcome injection of that untranslatable Danish 'hygge' to W10. Décor is, predictably, Scandinavian minimalist: white walls, nice wood floors, a few splashes of royal blue and, of course, Eames chairs and Poulsen lights. The open rye sandwiches (smørrebrød) are simple but perfected to a tee, the rarebit (malt-soaked rye and Gamle Ole cheese) is tangy yet comforting in all the right ways and, while the cinnamon buns aren't the best in London (for those head to the Scandinavian Kitchen, see p63 or Nordic Bakery, see p110), the flat white is definitely a contender for a crown.

—

93 Golborne Road, W10 5NL.
020 8964 3004
www.snapsandrye.com
Ladbroke Grove tube.

✹ BIRDHOUSE

Despite stiff competition from the cafés surrounding Clapham Junction (the excellent Story Coffee is just a few doors down), this Cuban-run outfit has built a deserved fanbase thanks to its passionately sourced beans and flavour-packed brunches and lunches. Forget chintzy teacups; Birdhouse's modern-municipal décor mixes reclaimed school desks, slate-grey walls and filament bulbs, plus clusters of kooky bird-themed artwork. Nothing is slapdash: a single-origin coffee menu complements the Climpson & Sons house blend, while a splendid range of fresh, creative food options namecheck top-quality suppliers such as Brindisa. Cuban specialities abound, with ropa vieja, bocaditos (sandwiches loaded with anything from steak, caramelised onions and cheddar to chicken, bacon jam and cabbage) and even mojitos featuring on the menu. The cool, upbeat vibe has proved a local hit.

—

123 St John's Hill, SW11 1SZ.
020 7228 6663
www.birdhou.se
Clapham Junction Overground.

✷ BIRDIE NUM NUMS

The achingly hip attendees of Goldsmiths college (just over the road from Birdie Num Nums) adore this café for two reasons. First, the interior: a charming mish-mash of rustic knick-knacks, Anatolian bazaar tat and red leather armchairs make it a lovely place to sip fruit tea and flick though a well-thumbed Balzac. Second, the menu: homely classics like fish finger sandwiches and giant baked jacket potatoes satisfyingly fill the void left by mummy's cooking, enhanced by nifty, playful grown-up touches (for instance the 'pulled-pork mac 'n' cheese'). In a nod to history (the space has been looked after by the same Turkish family for three generations), the café also fries a mean falafel, and a novel 'full Turkish' breakfast with chargrilled halloumi, red pepper hummus, olives and buttered, sesame-dusted corek bread.

—

11 Lewisham Way, SE14 6PP.
020 8692 7223
www.birdienumnums.co.uk
New Cross Overground.

✺ MONOCLE

Many a café can be described as looking like it's leapt from the pages of a lifestyle magazine, but this sleek-lined Marylebone hotspot actually has – it was set up by the founder of both cult design mag Wallpaper* and niche, hipster-leaning, global-affairs publication Monocle. With this pedigree, it's no surprise that it's a favourite with the style crowd. That it looks ultra-chic is (likewise) a no-brainer, but the café also delivers brilliantly on the food front, mixing Japanese and Scandi influences in snacks, breakfast and lunch, such as a sandwich filled with crunchy shrimp katsu or a filling chicken nanban. To drink, try an Allpress coffee or the much-Instagrammed matcha hot chocolate. Or make like a Monocle subscriber and pop in for an Aperol spritz.

—

18 Chiltern St, W1U 7QA.
020 7135 2040
cafe.monocle.com
Baker Street or Bond Street tube.

MONOCLE

✳ CAFÉ VIVA

Viva put down roots in Peckham before the area became trendy, and the low-key venue has become a locals' favourite thanks to its wholesome food and lovely staff. The very compact, lived-in interior (bare brick plastered with flyers on one side, white walls showcasing Peckham-based artists on the other, an open kitchen at the back, and a mish-mash of artfully battered secondhand chairs and tables in-between), welcomes a combination of freelancers, families and passing flâneurs. Specials such as subtly spiced lentil, spinach and coconut soup are excellent additions to a menu that focusses on all-day breakfasty snacks such as brioche baps filled with chorizo, fried egg, roasted tomatoes and rocket. To finish, the carrot, mango and coconut cake is a moist and fruity foil to a fortifying cup of locally roasted Volcano coffee.

—

44 Choumert Road, SE15 4SE.
020 7639 2922
www.cafeviva.co.uk
Peckham Rye Overground.

IVY'S
MESS HALL

✷ IVY'S MESS HALL

This café's green and white striped awning is like a beacon guiding Dalston's peace-cravers toward a haven away from the chaos of Kingsland Road. Inside, it's effortlessly and rustically chic: dark wooden floorboards and exposed brick walls are a backdrop to worn wooden tables, metal stools and bible-pocket chairs. Massive pastries, homemade cakes and generous sandwiches adorn the stainless steel bar (all modestly priced), but a proper meal is worth settling in for. Rotating daily specials include morning burritos and chorizo and avocado brioche buns, a series of exciting small plates, beautifully cooked steak and lots of lovely things delivered on artisan toast. Food (and cocktails) are served well into the evening, when the dusky den takes on the vibe of a stylishly dishevelled candlelit café-bar from the backstreets of Berlin.

—

129 Kingsland Road, E8 2PB.
020 7254 8006
No website.
Dalston Junction or Dalston Kingsland Overground.

✷ SPIT JACKS

With its bright yellow front, it's impossible to miss Spit Jacks, which is sat in the heart of Hackney's lovely little Victoria Park Village. Although it's known for its buttermilk fried chicken, most of the menu is Spanish-flavoured – think tortilla or Serrano ham and manchego sandwiches for lunch, and tapas for dinner. The Iberian influence even extends to breakfast – why have a full English when you can try huevos rancheros (eggs with black beans and salsa) or huevos rotos (eggs with chorizo and fries)? It's not easy to get to (there's no nearby station) but since it's on the edge of Victoria Park, you can weave a Spit Jacks stop into your exploration of the area.

—

87 Lauriston Road, E9 7HJ.
0208 985 7773
www.spitjacks.co.uk
London Fields or Cambridge Heath Overground.

SEVEN MORE

- **TANYA'S CAFÉ**
  Raw, vegan, organic, ethical, gluten- and dairy-free superfoods in a Chelsea hotspot that's somehow more hip than hippyish.
  35 Ixworth Place, SW3 3QX. South Kensington tube.

- **NANNA'S**
  Looks like your gran's house circa 1976, but thankfully the menu of smoothies, toasties and cakes are thoroughly modern.
  274b St Paul's Road, N1 2LJ. Highbury & Islington tube.

- **SCANDINAVIAN KITCHEN**
  Busy central café and grocery shop for all your Nordic needs – cinammon buns, beetroot salads, herring and lots of rye bread.
  61 Great Titchfield Street, W1W 7PP. Oxford Circus tube.

- **TOTA**
  A smart Tooting café that does brunch, lunch and dinner with panache and emphasises rigorous sourcing.
  102 Tooting High Street, SW17 0RR. Tooting Broadway tube.

- **THE GOOD LIFE EATERY**
  Hemp, chia, quinoa, kale – if it's healthy it's here. Without ever getting ascetic, this chic café does wellness in style.
  59 Sloane Avenue, SW3 3DH. Sloane Square tube.

- **BEL & NEV**
  Super-friendly local café run by two experienced chefs – almost everything is cooked in-house. And it's all good.
  15 Station Terrace, NW10 5RX. Kensal Rise Overground.

- **BLUE BRICK CAFÉ (pictured)**
  A cosy little corner bistro with a varied vegetarian menu of homely dishes: chickpea stew, soup and veggie curry.
  14 Fellbrigg Road, SE22 9HH. East Dulwich rail.

You only have to turn the corner to stumble across yet another coffee shop declaring it makes the best brew in London. Take the risk out of your ristretto and head straight to these tried-and-approved caffeine-loving cafés.

COFFEE

✷ THE WATCH HOUSE

Built in the early 1800s as a guardhouse for the nearby St Mary Magdalene churchyard (quite what it was guarding, or from whom, is unclear), The Watch House is now a small but perfectly-formed café that's emblematic of the artisanal renaissance Bermondsey has experienced in the last few years. The coffee is justifiably lauded as the best in the postcode; the lattes are spot-on, and there's a bottomless single-origin fresh brew that's perfect for the wifi hoggers who set up camp here in the daytime. Sandwiches, baguettes and salads are amply proportioned and all made onsite with fresh, organic and locally sourced ingredients. Best of all is the décor: distressed brickwork, exposed beams and a recessed bench area for conspiratorial chinwags.

—

193 Bermondsey Street, SE1 3UW.

No phone.

www.watchhousecoffee.com

Borough or Bermondsey tube.

ALMOND MILK £0.30P
SERVED DOUBLE SHOT AS STANDARD
MADE WITH ORGANIC MILK
Lemon and poppyseed Loaf £2.00

TUTORING

✷ HEJ

Aside from the name, which is Swedish for 'hello', Hej is Scandi without hitting you over the head with it – the décor is understated, the space light and airy, thanks to beautiful big windows. You'll want to linger over delicious cinnamon buns and cheekily titled 'Viking Balls', or muffins, brownies, salmon bagels and cheddar scones. The coffee (made with beans from Swedish coffee company Löfbergs) is strong with no hint of bitterness. And there's plenty of room to be leisurely about the whole thing, though the seats in the window are often taken by freelancers and students on laptops. The only thing that may threaten to cut your stay short is the lack of a toilet.

—

1 Bermondsey Square, SE1 3UN.
No phone.
www.hejcoffee.co.uk
London Bridge or Borough tube.

✸ CLIMPSON & SONS

Broadway Market stretches in a graceful arc from London Fields to Regent's Canal, and is a mecca for artisan food lovers lured by its many speciality stallholders every Saturday. As you might expect, there's no shortage of places to grab a fancy cup of coffee, but Climpson & Sons is unequivocally the best. It was founded by Ian Burgess, an industrious chap so impressed by the coffee he sampled travelling in Australia that he set up his own London stall in the early noughties. By the end of the decade Climpson & Sons had grown into a coffee roaster and bona fide bricks-and-mortar East End institution. A nice illustration of its famous attention to detail: if you take sugar, baristas will add it at the espresso stage, so as not to ruin the silky foam finish. A class act.

—

67 Broadway Market, E8 4PH.
020 7812 9829
www.climpsonandsons.com
London Fields Overground.

✷ BULLDOG EDITION AT ACE HOTEL

For as pure and perfect a hipster experience as you could wish for, stop by this barista paradise in the lobby of the Ace Hotel on Shoreditch High Street. The staff go to an awful lot of trouble over the coffee. Beans hail from Square Mile Coffee Roasters, with World Tasters Champion Anette Moldvaer setting the brewing standard, while the milk comes from the happy grazers of Northiam Dairy on the Kent/Sussex border. This might seem a faff over nothing, but the proof is in the tasting: a nuttier, sweeter latte, and a foam as sleek and tantalising as the models sipping on their green tea. There's also excellent filter coffees, beautiful pastries and soup and sandwiches for lunch – you might have to grab-and-go though, as there's limited window-side seating.

—

100 Shoreditch High Street, E1 6JQ.
020 7613 9800
www.acehotel.com
Shoreditch High Street Overground.

✷ ALCHEMY

If there's anyone in London who needs caffeine, it's City workers, and this trendy set-up in the heart of the Square Mile delivers a top-quality hit. Alchemy's café is kitted out with wooden counters, filament bulbs and white walls adorned with only a blackboard menu – it may sound awfully familiar, but it's a breath of fresh air among the City's soulless chains. With real heart, the owners trade directly with plantation owners in Central and South America, bringing the beans to their south London roastery. The list of traditional espresso-based coffees is backed up by more modish offerings such as cold brews and excellent filter coffees (there's loads of brewing equipment available to buy too). Snacks range from cakes including raspberry and nectarine friands to more ample lunch options – but nothing that will detract from the star of the show. In a word: magic.

—

8 Ludgate Broadway, EC4V 6DU.
020 7329 9904
www.alchemycoffee.co.uk
Blackfriars tube or City Thameslink rail.

✺ THE FIELDS BENEATH

Nestled in the base of an old Victorian viaduct (right next to Kentish Town West Overground), this intimate coffee bar and snackery is small in size but giant in reputation. Named after local antiquarian Gillian Tindall's landmark 1977 study of Kentish Town's history, it's become a neighbourhood institution in a postcode which prides itself on togetherness. Queuing up for one of its magnificent coffees (for ages the café operated a rotating supplier policy, but have lately settled on a fruitful collaboration with Coffee by Tate, which roasts its wares in a WWII Nissen hut in the grounds of Tate Britain), you'll tune in to all manner of juicy local gossip. By the time you've polished off your toastie, croissant or cheeringly gigantic cookie and slurped the last of your macchiato, you'll wish you lived nearby yourself.

—

52a Prince of Wales Road, NW5 3LN.
020 7424 8838
No website.
Kentish Town West Overground.

✷ PRUFROCK

You might expect this spacious, well-situated establishment to be a bit full of itself, given that its name is a reference to a TS Eliot poem, the director is a former World Barista Champion, and that it currently teaches internationally-accredited courses in the fine art of coffee. Not a bit of it. The staff are as lively, likeable and lovely as the coffee they serve. The weekday denizens are mostly local creatives and tech entrepreneurs, many of whom tend to appreciate the finer things, so not only is the espresso without comparison, the food is far, far more ambitious than your usual coffee shop fare. Try a pork belly, chorizo and bean stew, or a stellar haddock kedgeree.

—

23-25 Leather Lane, EC1N 7TE.
020 7242 0467
www.prufrockcoffee.com
Farringdon or Chancery Lane tube.

CHEMEX
CHEMEX

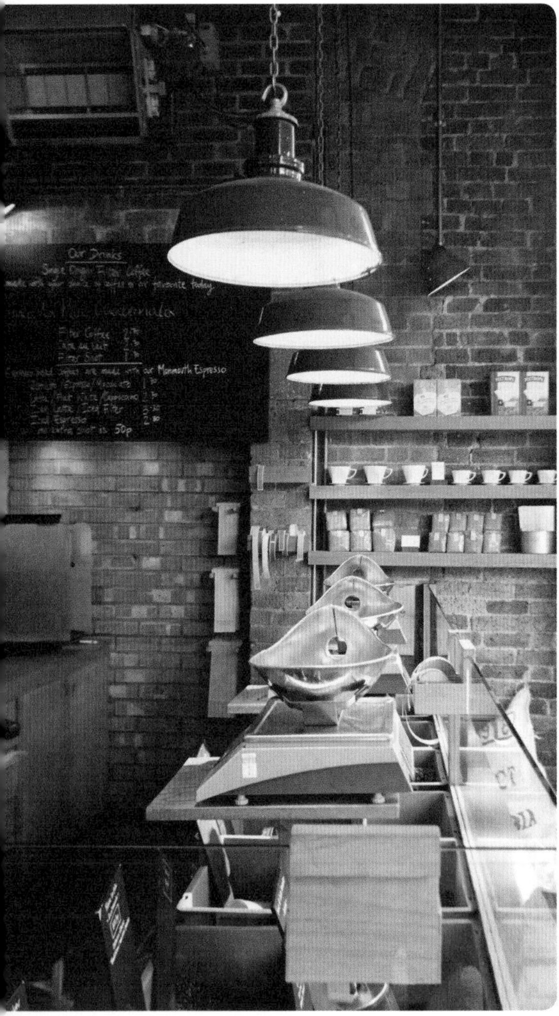
Our Drinks
Monmouth Espresso
50p

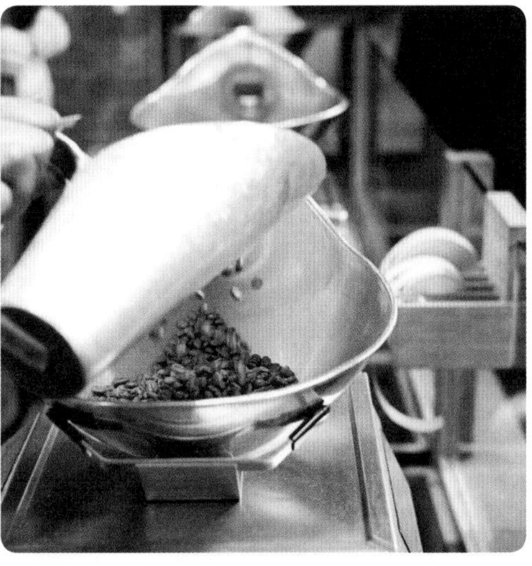

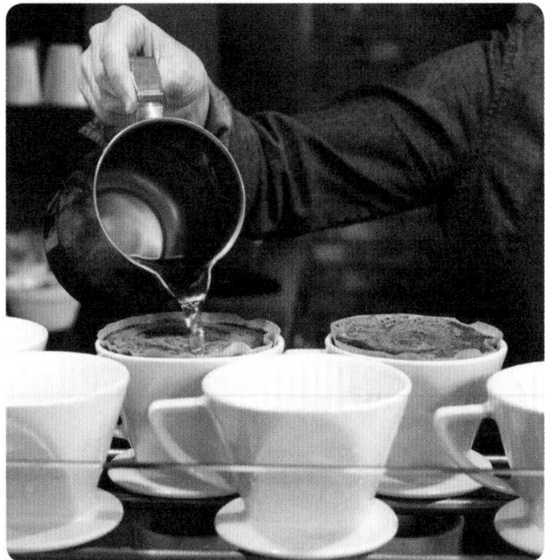

✷ MONMOUTH

The folks at Monmouth started their obsession with sourcing and roasting high-quality, sustainable coffee beans back in 1978, decades before most Londoners could even pronounce 'espresso' correctly. The capital's caffeine scene has come a long way since then, but Monmouth still leads the way. Its regularly changing selection of fairly traded, single-origin beans are roasted at the company's Bermondsey headquarters and served as filter coffee. Go for the tart, chocolatey Guatemalan Finca la Pila, or the sweet, fruity Ethiopian Deri Kojao. If you don't spot the queue snaking from this prime corner site, you'll smell the beans – staff spend all day shovelling them whole into bags or grinding them for customers to buy, or to enjoy in the farmhouse-style café area as they soak up Borough Market's atmosphere.

—

2 Park Street, SE1 9AB.
020 7232 3010
www.monmouthcoffee.co.uk
London Bridge tube.
BRANCHES: Covent Garden WC2H 9EU; Bermondsey SE16 4EJ.

✷ TIMBERYARD

This café is an unofficial office for the laptop-toting twentysomethings who take up residence on its comfortable sofas to tap away as they get their caffeine and sugar fixes. The former comes courtesy of Has Bean roastery – try a toasty, aromatic latte or, if time allows, the superior buzz of a drip-fed, slow-brewed 'Chemex for two'. Timberyard's sweet treats don't pull their punches, either: gargantuan slices of peanut butter loaf cake, glossy wedges of raspberry and almond tart, and salted-caramel brownies are all must-trys. The savoury selection is no less mouthwatering, with deep-filled quiches and wax-paper-wrapped sandwiches, toasted to order. Timberyard's secret weapon, however, is its staff, whose friendly, feel-good approach takes the sting out of the inevitable queues and hustle for a seat.

—

7 Upper St Martin's Lane, WC2H 9DL.
No phone.
www.timberyardlondon.com
Leicester Square tube.
BRANCHES: Old Street EC1V 9HW.

✸ SHOREDITCH GRIND

The suave brick cylinder on the rim of the recently rebranded 'Silicon Roundabout' (Old Street roundabout, to you and me) was the first in the chain of 'Grinds', with outlets now in Soho, Holborn and London Bridge. The key to its success is more than a great coffee – notably a legendary flat white, alongside shorter offerings such as a piccolo and macchiato. It also has tasty bites (the moist, moreish rosemary focaccia bookends some lovely sandwiches), cocktails in the evenings, and an insistent, pumping soundtrack. The music is entirely central to the operation: co-founder Kaz was one half of Bodyrockers ('I like the way you move') and their upstairs recording suite has committed to tape the dulcet tones of the likes of Sam Smith, Pixie Lott and Tinie Tempah.

—

213 Old Street, EC1V 9NR.
020 7490 7490
www.shoreditchgrind.com
Old Street tube.
BRANCHES: Soho W1F 9RP; Holborn WC1V 7BD; London Bridge SE1 9RA.

✷ BAR TERMINI

Bar Termini conjures up the ideal Italian station café (the one you'd describe to your friends ad nauseum when you got home) so convincingly that it would feel like a theme café if it wasn't so classy. Established by Tony Conigliaro, the Midas of London's cocktail-bar scene, it's a bijou space with pale green leather banquettes, shiny walnut tables, storage racks on bare-brick walls, and a marble-topped bar where coffees and cocktails are dispensed with equal care and attention. The latte is a triple measure of the peerlessly smooth house coffee, expressed as a double ristretto and served in a Continental-style bowl with a jug of foamy milk (a blend of two milks). Snacks include Italian-style croissants, bite-sized filled rolls and charcuterie. It's a perfect fit for villagey Soho.

—

7 Old Compton Street, W1D 5JE.
07860 945 018
www.bar-termini.com
Leicester Square tube.

E61 Legend
FAEMA

✷ WORKSHOP

This cool customer has steadily made a name for itself since opening in 2011 – the term 'coffee shop' just doesn't do it justice. Sure, it takes coffee seriously: the on-site roastery filled with bags of painstakingly sourced beans, the house-roasted coffee on sale at the cake-laden counter, and the monogrammed, expertly manned La Marzocco coffee machine all attest to that (as do Workshop's smooth and savoury brews). But coffee is just one of the reasons why Clerkenwell's residents and workers regularly fill the tables in the stylish, low-lit, dining room. Workshop also offers stonking breakfasts and brunches (try the house take on huevos rancheros, topped with braised beans, jerk sauce and jalapeños), elegant lunch and dinner menus, and even cocktails. Cheery table service is another plus – if you can get a table, that is.

—

27 Clerkenwell Road, EC1M 5RN.
020 7253 5754
www.workshopcoffee.com
Farringdon tube.
BRANCHES: Fitzrovia W1W 7FE; Holborn EC1A 2FD; Marylebone W1U 1AX.

SEVEN MORE

- **TAP**
  A haven for serious coffee fiends (the pour over is faultless), but also a stop-off for superior cakes and simple breakfasts.
  Three branches, including 193 Wardour Street, W1F 8ZF. Oxford Circus tube.

- **DEPARTMENT OF COFFEE & SOCIAL AFFAIRS**
  Exemplary coffee, and it goes down easy knowing 'social affairs' means supporting humanitarian projects at home and abroad.
  Eight branches, including 14-16 Leather Lane, EC1N 7SU. Farringdon tube.

- **COFFEE CIRCUS (pictured)**
  More a cosy café than a classic coffee bar, Coffee Circus is still dedicated to top beans (and tea leaves) from around the world.
  136 Crouch Hill, N8 9DX. Crouch Hill Overground.

- **BAR ITALIA**
  Italian brews served via a Gaggia coffee machine in the retro surrounds of this Soho classic run by an Italian family since 1949.
  22 Frith Street, W1D 4RF. Tottenham Court Road tube.

- **DAILY GOODS**
  Filters with a refill and silky smooth cappuccinos, plus brilliant banana bread and Neal's Yard grilled cheese.
  36 Camberwell Church Street, SE5 8QZ. Denmark Hill Overground.

- **NUDE ESPRESSO**
  Nude's modern look happily belies its artisan ethos – everything is hand-done, from bean roasting to raisin-toast baking.
  26 Hanbury Street, E1 6QR. Shoreditch High Street Overground.

- **THE ESPRESSO ROOM**
  This tiny 'room' leaves no space for error or fripperies, focusing on outstanding espresso made with the best guest roasts.
  31-35 Great Ormond Street, WC1N 3HZ. Russell Square tube.

Sink your fork into the fluffiest carrot cake in town, or bite into a crisp, buttery croissant (that's easily as good as its Parisian counterparts), at one of these incredibly good cafés, cake shops and bakeries.

CAKES & BAKES

✷ HUMMINGBIRD BAKERY

Residents of well-heeled South Kensington are used to the best of everything. A stone's throw from the Natural History Museum, and a few doors down from a vast Lamborghini showroom, the Hummingbird Bakery is eminently worthy. Whether you fancy its renowned red velvet cake (people travel halfway across the world for this one), bubblegum-frosted rainbow cake or the frankly awesome humble pumpkin pie, you're assured a high-calibre sugar rush like no other. The attractively-tiled interior is inviting, but often chock-full. To minimise the stress of the hustle, arrive expecting to wait and hold out for a seat on the cute ballustraded front patio, the perfect spot for a post-museum breather.

—

47 Old Brompton Road, SW7 3JP.
020 7851 1795
www.hummingbirdbakery.com
South Kensington tube.
BRANCHES: Angel EC1V 4AB; Notting Hill W11 2DY; Richmond TW9 1BP; Soho W1F 8WG; Spitalfields E1 7HS.

✷ BAGERIET

This chic, serene and tiny Swedish café is located in a peaceful alley altogether removed from Covent Garden's unending bustle. Inside, neat rows of cinnamon- and caraway-laden cakes decorate the otherwise simply designed space, with its white-wood panelling and shelves stacked with crispbreads and jams. Among the sweet treats baked by Ottolenghi alumnus Daniel Karlsson are neat swirls of cinnamon buns, puffy sugared pretzels and icing-topped, almond-filled mazarin tarts. The choice stretches from the front door to the back counter, where princess cakes – domed, featherlight sponges filled with fresh cream and jam, a Nordic riff on Victoria sponge – take pride of place. In summer, the two outside tables are a secluded sun-trap where you can make-believe you've got London all to yourself.

—

24 Rose Street, WC2E 9EA.
020 7240 0000
www.bageriet.co.uk
Covent Garden tube.

✷ LA PÂTISSERIE DES RÊVES

The nicest thing about this boutique Parisian pâtisserie import, save perhaps for the incredible hazelnut Paris-Brest, is its authenticity: all the staff and at least 50 percent of the customers are French. An unassuming interior is dominated by a central table of pastries covered by glass domes. The old-favourites are there year-round, including millefeuille, chocolate-wrapped éclairs and seasonal fruit tarts, while 'collections' change throughout the year. Kids will love the Breton kouign amann, a caramelised, buttery pastry, which here is served on a stick – perfect for munching on the go (seating is outdoor only). Head down early on the weekend to be in with a chance of getting a croissant.

—

43 Marylebone High Street, W1U 5HE.
020 3603 7333
www.lapatisseriedesreves.com
Baker Street or Regent's Park tube.
BRANCHES: South Kensington SW7 2HE.

✷ BALTHAZAR BOULANGERIE

This little gem is often overlooked for its louder and roaringly popular elder brother, Balthazar Brasserie, next door. And what a shame that is. From the brushed gold walls and mosaic floors to the soft jazz soundtrack, the Boulangerie feels like a step back in time to 1920s Paris – albeit via a slightly circuitous route, since Balthazar is in fact an import of a French-inspired New York restaurant. The counter is laden with pastries and tarts, the best of which is the apple and hazelnut galette, and the coffee is dark and invigorating. Seating is limited to a small bar at the window. A little haven from the tourist rush of Covent Garden, and with far more heart than its sibling restaurant.

—

4-6 Russell Street, WC2B 5HZ.
020 3301 1155
www.balthazarlondon.com
Covent Garden tube.

✷ ST JOHN MALTBY

In a characteristically straightforward style, the bakery set up by the St John group to supply its restaurants (and others) with bread, old-school baked desserts and cakes, sells direct to in-the-know foodies from a heaving trestle table located at 72 Druid Street (the St John Bakery) every Saturday morning. Around the corner, you'll also find Maltby Street's weekend market and St John's second local destination, St John Maltby, open Wednesday to Sunday. Here, the aforementioned cakes are served alongside coffee, by-the-glass wines and snacky savoury dishes in a pared-back setting. What you'll hear people chatting about (and queuing for) at both locations, though, are St John's signature doughnuts (generously filled with fresh vanilla custard or seasonal fruit jam), sensational Eccles cakes and madeleines so popular that fresh batches are baked every hour.

—

41 Maltby Street, SE1 2PA.
020 7553 9844
www.stjohngroup.uk.com
London Bridge tube.

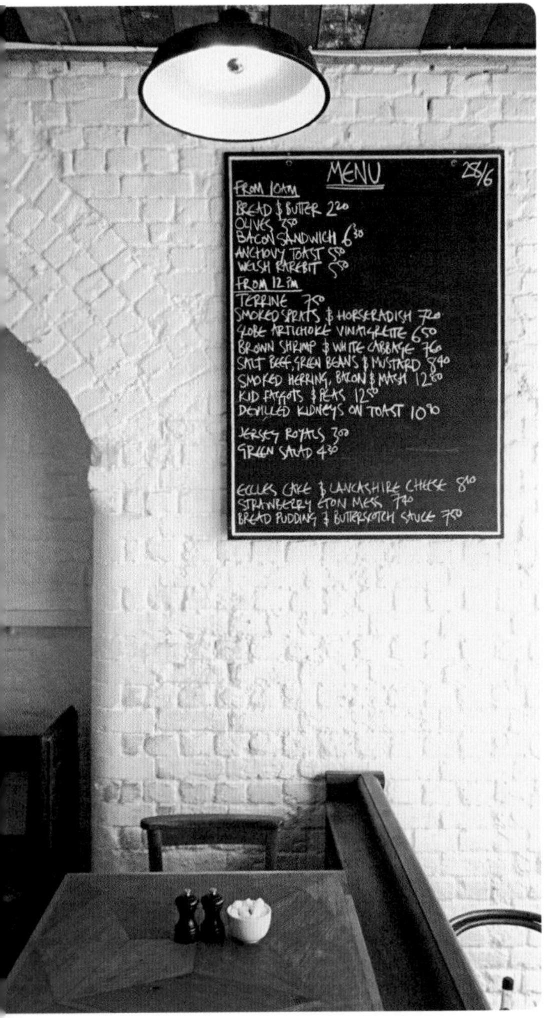
MENU
28/6
FROM 10AM
BREAD & BUTTER 2.20
OLIVES 3.50
BACON SANDWICH 6.30
ANCHOVY TOAST 5.50
WELSH RAREBIT 5.50
FROM 12 PM
TERRINE 7.50
SMOKED SPRATS & HORSERADISH 7.20
GLOBE ARTICHOKE VINAIGRETTE 6.50
BROWN SHRIMP & WHITE CABBAGE 7.60
SALT BEEF, GREEN BEANS & MUSTARD 8.40
SMOKED HERRING, BACON & MASH 12.80
KID FAGGOTS & PEAS 12.50
DEVILLED KIDNEYS ON TOAST 10.80
JERSEY ROYALS 3.00
GREEN SALAD 4.30
ECCLES CAKE & LANCASHIRE CHEESE 8.10
STRAWBERRY ETON MESS 7.40
BREAD PUDDING & BUTTERSCOTCH SAUCE 7.50

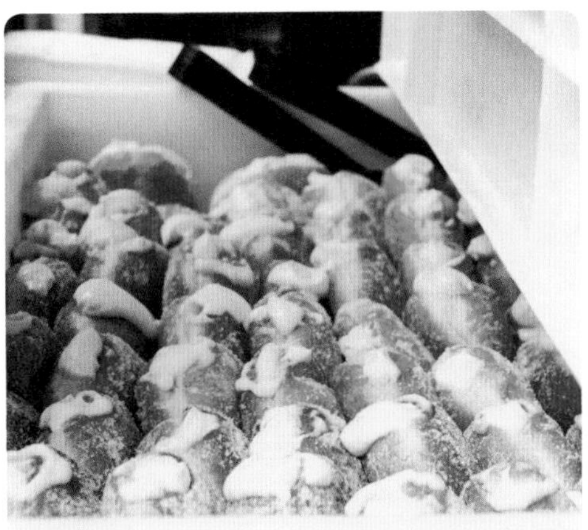

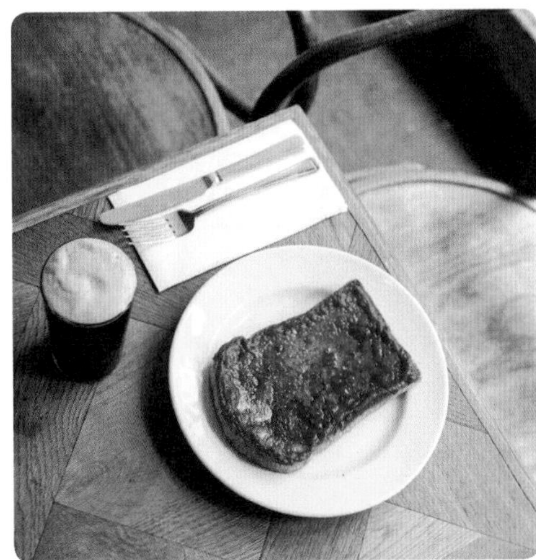

MAISON BERTAUX
28 PATISSERIE FRANCAISE
ON BERTAUX
ated Tea Rooms Patisserie Française
MAISON BERT
Creating Daily on the Premises Est

✳ MAISON BERTAUX

Established in 1871, Maison Bertaux has stubbornly refused to modernise and is all the better for it. The coffee is old-fashioned, but decent, the gateaux St-Honore heavenly, the fruit tarts some of the best in London, and it's as far from a coffee chain as is humanly possible – all of which more than excuses the chaotic service and décor that is more shabby than chic. The striped blue awning and tables on the pavement (come rain or shine) look thoroughly European and its slightly shambolic eccentricity gives it a feeling of being off the beaten track, despite its location firmly wedged between Theatreland and the chaos of Oxford Street. This is a little slice of timelessness in ever-evolving Soho.

—

28 Greek Street, W1D 5DQ.
020 7437 6007
www.maisonbertaux.com
Leicester Square tube.

✳ KONDITOR & COOK

If a cake could ever be described as 'cult', Konditor's Curly Whirly Cake would surely be it: a dark chocolate sponge layered with vanilla buttercream and decorated with frosting and signature dark chocolate ganache swirls. Other treats include a moist and not-too-sweet lemon chiffon and the incredible wheat-free chocolate noisette cake: chocolate and hazelnut sponges layered with gianduja mascarpone icing. The Waterloo branch is where founder Gerhard Jenne first started the mini-chain in 1993 and it has plenty of character, including a beautiful purple Victorian shopfront and charmingly uneven wooden floors inside. The coffee is good, but the hot chocolate – with double cream and the finest Callebaut – is truly wicked.

—

22 Cornwall Road, SE1 8TW.
020 7633 3333
www.konditorandcook.com
Waterloo tube.

BRANCHES: Borough Market SE1 9AD; Chancery Lane WC1X 8LR; The Gherkin EC3A 8BF; Goodge Street W1T 2PX; Spitalfields E1 6DT.

✷ SOUTHERDEN

Next to the towering heights of the Shard, the modest proportions of foodie mecca Bermondsey Street feel almost quaint. Southerden stands out, not least for its optical illusion-like wallpaper, designed by Eley Kishimoto. The menu here is in a constant process of reinvention (owner Mel's Michelin-starred roots are clear) and you'll find some exceptionally forward-thinking cakes among the classics. Start with a Chouxmert Bun – a choux bun filled with crème pâtissière and finished with a crumble topping, which is Mel's own mad and mouthwatering invention – then grab a cup of Monmouth and keep on eating. The unlikely-sounding devilled egg and avocado éclairs are incredible, as is the timeless lemon meringue tart. While you're in the area, the St John Bakery and Bakery Rooms (see p90) is the place for a fat jam doughnut.

—

72 Bermondsey Street, SE1 3UD.
020 7378 1585
www.southerden.com
London Bridge tube.

VIOLET
BANANA AND
BUTTERMILK
SLICE

✷ VIOLET CAKES

A cosy, homey aesthetic belies the calibre of cake on offer at this Hackney-based café, owned by Californian Claire Ptak, previously at Chez Panisse in the US. The ground floor is dominated by the open kitchen and bags of flour crammed into every available space, with seating largely on the pavement and upstairs on large communal tables. Commuters pile in for cinnamon buns at breakfast and a slice of the daily quiche or sandwich at lunch, but the real stand-out are the cakes. The salted chocolate caramel is delicious, as is the buttermilk banana bread, and the icing on the vanilla cupcakes changes with the seasons: rhubarb in the spring, fragola grapes in the autumn and red berries in the summer.

—

47 Wilton Way, E8 3ED.
020 7275 8360
www.violetcakes.com
Hackney Central Overground.

✻ PRINCI

The sleek elegance of Alan Yau (Hakkasan, The Duck and Rice) and Italian baker Rocco Princi's all-day café-pizzeria – which combines acres of marble, high communal tables, plate-glass frontage, and even a trickling water feature – make it ideal for informal meetings, casual dates or an unhurried lunch with the girls. Although the extensive menu includes Italian-style cooked breakfasts, pizza by the slice, filled focaccia and multi-coloured salads, Princi's pièce de résistance is its long counter displaying tray upon tray of picture-perfect pâtisserie: hazelnut-and-chocolate sponge topped with creamy praline; jewel-like fruit tarts; sugar-dusted, custard-filled millefoglie and individual tiramisus, plus freshly baked breads. The chic continental vibe is heightened by efficient, uniformed staff in jaunty white caps. To drink, try a glass of wine from the sizeable all-Italian list. Just bear in mind it gets busy in here. Really busy.

—

135 Wardour Street, W1F 0UT.
020 7478 8888
www.princi.com
Oxford Circus tube.

✷ PRIMROSE BAKERY

What Carrie Bradshaw and the Magnolia Bakery did for cupcakes in New York, the Primrose Bakery did for London. The original branch is small, but undisputedly the best. It has everything you could want from a seller of sugar and sprinkles: a combination of American diner and English tea room that is neither tacky nor twee; mint green walls that match the beautiful jadeite milk glass cake stands; and sponges with just the right cake-to-icing ratio. The chocolate bar-inspired cupcakes are the best (when available), while the peanut butter flavour is without equal. If you want to get a look-in (and a seat), avoid the school-rush hours, when kids from the local primary school descend to cover their faces in chocolate cake.

—

69 Gloucester Avenue, NW1 8LD.
020 7483 4222
www.primrose-bakery.co.uk
Chalk Farm tube.
BRANCHES: Covent Garden WC2E 7PB;
Kensington W14 8NZ.

✷ PEGGY PORSCHEN

Peggy Porschen's cake emporium is easy to spot on Ebury Street – its bubblegum-pink façade stands out amid the grown-up shops and smart townhouses, and the windows showcasing its stunning three-tiered cakes (posh wedding towers are a speciality) draw oohs and aahs from passers-by. The interior can only be described as 'girly': a sea of pink and white with pastel-coloured crockery, jars of floral teas and decorative tissue-paper pom-poms. Exquisite cakes range from banoffee cupcakes with perfectly piped icing, walnut-flecked sponge and a liquid caramel centre to regal three-layer sandwich cakes such as strawberry and champagne (topped with pink truffles), or darkly glossy salted caramel. Staff are as sweet as the delicacies they serve. For true enthusiasts, Peggy Porschen's cake academy – pink, naturally – is across the street.

—

116 Ebury Street, SW1W 9QQ.
020 7730 1316
www.peggyporschen.com
Sloane Square tube.

PEGGY PORSCHEN
LOVE LAYER CAKES
NEW BOOK!
LOVE LAYER CAKES
BY PEGGY PORSCHEN
30 EXCLUSIVE RECIPES

✷ E5 BAKEHOUSE

Clapton-dweller Ben Mackinnon swapped a corporate career for baking back in 2011, and soon found himself running a much-loved café and bakery school. Tucked under a railway arch by London Fields station, E5 Bakehouse has shelves stacked with loaves and a huge selection of cakes and pastries which have all been baked that day, from carrot cake to croissants. For a peek behind the scenes, head to the loo – you'll have to meander through the kitchen, where you can see dough being kneaded and huge trays of baguettes being proved. The compact café only has a few tables and does tend to get busy, so if you can't find a space, opt for takeaway and enjoy it alfresco in London Fields.

—

Arch 395, Mentmore Terrace, E8 3PH.
020 8986 9600
www.e5bakehouse.com
London Fields Overground.

396

✳ FABRIQUE

Cinnamon buns are a Swedish institution, and London's best can arguably be found at Fabrique, along with their delicious close cousins, cardamom buns, and an array of sweet treats and breads fresh from the stone oven. Fabrique started out as a bakery in Stockholm's hip Södermalm district and expended to a chain of 11 before hopping across the North Sea for its London debut under a railway arch in Hoxton. This outpost is more than a little reminiscent of E5 Bakehouse (see p102), with its rustic bare brick, tin roof and just a handful of tables, but inexplicably, it's not nearly as busy. So you'll be able to enjoy your fika (coffee break) in peace, complete with a brew made using beans from Swedish roasters Johan & Nyström.

—

Arch 385, Geffrye Street, E2 8HZ.
020 7033 0268
www.fabrique.co.uk
Hoxton Overground.
BRANCHES: Covent Garden WC2H 9RY.

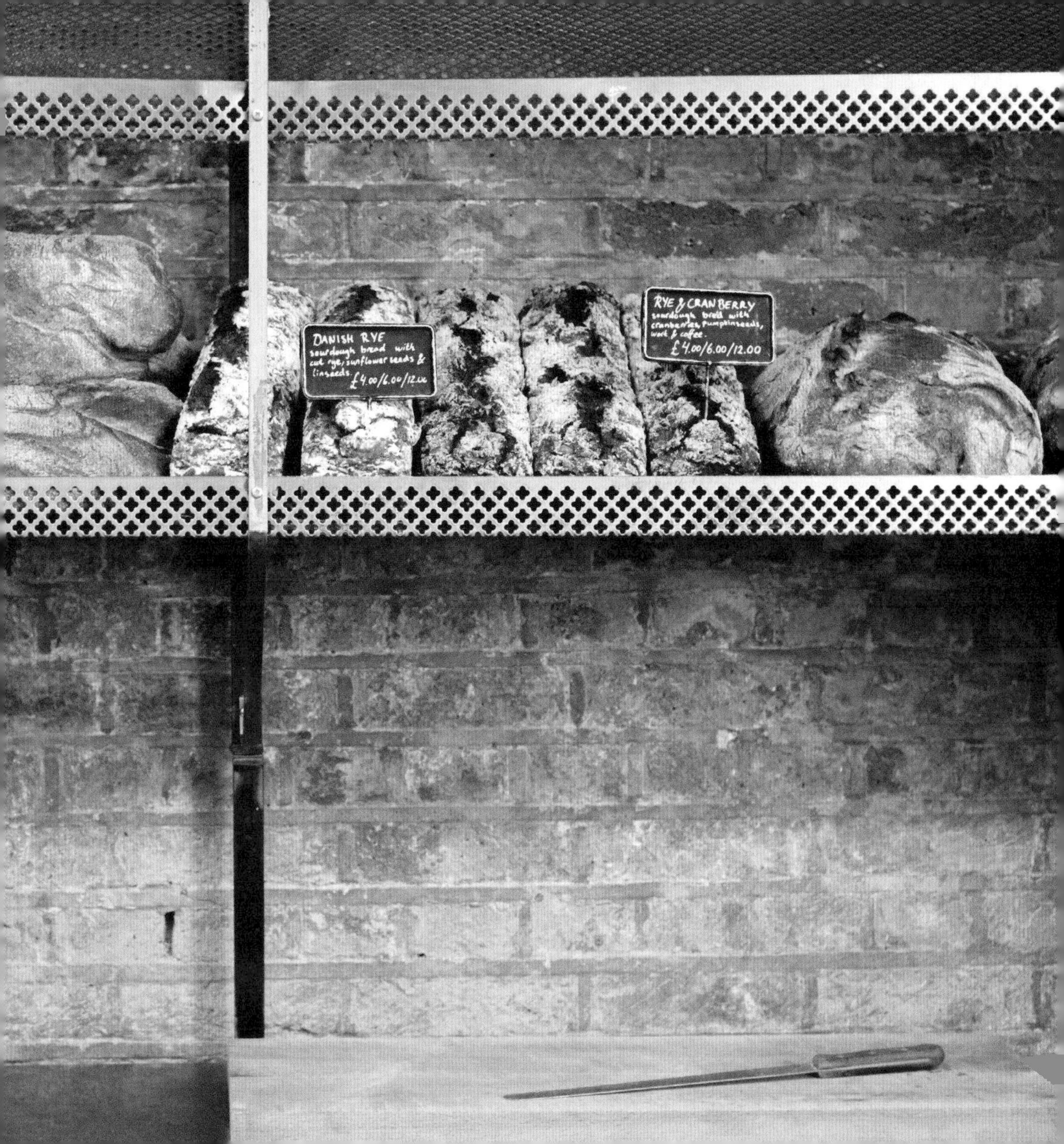
DANISH RYE
sourdough bread with
cut rye, sunflower seeds &
linseeds.
£4.00/6.00/12.00
RYE & CRANBERRY
sourdough bread with
cranberries, pumpkinseeds,
wort & coffee.
£4.00/6.00/12.00

LILY VANILLI

Hidden away in a pretty courtyard behind Columbia Road, this artisan bakery opens for just eight hours a week to coincide with the flower market on a Sunday. Lily is known for her sculptural and at times macabre bespoke cakes, and her offering is a much-needed antidote for those who have been out-butter-creamed and out-cutesied by the never ending cupcake craze. The bakes here are a brilliant balance of sweet and savoury, with flavour combinations including pear, thyme and olive oil, and courgette and beetroot, with extra lunch options including crisp and fat sausage rolls. String lights and a thick wood counter lend a rustic feel, but space is tight with just two communal tables (one inside, one out) and a bar, so expect to wait.

—

6 The Courtyard, Ezra Street, E2 7RH.
No phone.
www.lilyvanilli.com
Hoxton Overground.

✸ MOUSE & DE LOTZ

Owners Nadya Mousawi and Victoria de Lotz bake the kind of cakes and biscuits you wish your nan could whip up, and they serve them in what could be your nan's ultra-chic farmhouse. Settle in with a perfect flat white and a toasted teacake, or go for a white chocolate and raspberry tart, or a slice from one of the soft and bouncy sponges. There are vegan and gluten-free baked options too, and the lunch and brunch menus are equally thought through. Lovely things on toast (smoked salmon and horseradish; roast mushrooms and warm goat's cheese) join bright salads and fat sandwiches. A calm and cosy place to spend an afternoon.

—

103 Shacklewell Lane, E8 2EB.
020 3489 8082
www.mousedelotz.com
Dalston Kingsland Overground.

✷ WA CAFÉ

If you thought the French were the undisputed masters of fancy-pants pâtisserie, think again – the Japanese have become adept at applying French techniques to Far Eastern flavours with typical precision and perfectionism. This Ealing independent – a light-filled, minimalist space decked out in creamy shades of cappuccino with the odd glint of gold – is a prime example. The most popular cakes are airy choux pastries filled with 'shu cream' (crème pâtissière flavoured with, say, sesame or green tea). However, find room for savoury bakes such as deep-fried doughnuts filled with subtly spiced Japanese curry, or glazed bread rolls topped with teriyaki chicken. Wa is a one-off – for now – that has been embraced by locals, particularly mums who need a matcha latte pick-me-up before the school run.

---

32 Haven Green, W5 2NX.
020 8991 7855
www.wacafe.co.uk
Ealing Broadway tube.

NORDIC BAKERY

'Dark rye bread', 'cinnamon buns' and 'coffee' are the trio of enticers emblazoned on the window of this café – coupled with the cinnamon aroma wafting out of the door, they succeed in luring you in. Once inside you'll feel like you've travelled to one of the Nordic countries: there's the calming blue-grey colour scheme, stylish hardwood furniture by regional designers and an effortless sense of cool. Sandwiches are earthy and authentic, including pickled mustard herring with eggs and a richly smoky salmon on rye. And those wonderful, heavy, filling cinnamon buns are made using a Finnish recipe that's so good the brick-sized rolls tend to sell out by 11am. If you happen to be near the Soho branch on a nice morning, get one to go and perch outside in Golden Square.

—

37b New Cavendish Street, W1G 8JR.
020 7935 3590
www.nordicbakery.com
Baker Street or Regent's Park tube.
BRANCHES: Marylebone W1U 7NE; Soho W1F 9JG.

SEVEN MORE

- **CAKE BOY (pictured)**
  French patissier Eric Lanlard's fabulous pastries, cakes and tarts can be enjoyed with bubbles at this 'cake boutique'.
  Kingfisher House, Juniper Drive, SW18 1TX. Wandsworth Town rail.

- **CAKE ME BABY**
  A smart, peaceful café with inventive bakes, plus made-to-order cakes in the shape of anything from a monkey to a mohawk.
  163 Askew Road, W12 9AU. Goldhawk Road tube.

- **RINKOFF**
  This family-run bakery has been going since 1911, but keeps it contemporary with 'crodoughs' among the bagels and cakes.
  224 Jubilee Street, E1 3BS. Whitechapel or Stepney Green tube.

- **ARTISAN GLUTEN FREE BAKERY**
  No suprises: just good gluten-free bread and sweet treats, plus proper breakfast and lunch menus for the gluten-intolerent.
  167 Upper Street, N1 1US. Angel tube.

- **PAVILION BAKERY**
  A traditional bakery store front tempts you into Pavilion where stacks of just-baked bread and pastries call out your name.
  18 Broadway Market, E8 4QJ. Cambridge Heath Overground.

- **CUTTER & SQUIDGE**
  The sisters behind Cutter & Squidge serve incredible 'all natural' layer cakes, plus 'biskies' – a sort of biscuit-cake-frosting dream.
  20 Brewer Street, W1F 0SJ. Piccadilly Circus tube.

- **PÂTISSERIE SAINTE ANNE**
  The owners of this charming pâtisserie hopped over from Paris bringing brilliant baguettes, croissants and tarts with them.
  204 King Street, W6 0RA. Ravenscourt Park tube.

Some of London's finest hotels have been perfecting the art of afternoon tea for well over a century, while the city's modern establishments have learnt from the best. So whether you want a classic experience, or a contemporary take on tradition, these destinations should fit the bill.

AFTERNOON TEA

✷ BEA'S OF BLOOMSBURY

The original Bea's (in, yes, Bloomsbury) describes its afternoon tea as 'no frills', though 'laid-back' might be a better label. It's a description that could extend to the space itself, which is informal at the Bloomsbury branch, and only marginally more refined in the Farringdon and St Paul's offshoots. But Bea's is all about the very modestly priced cake stand, which comes stacked with scones, cupcakes, brownies, meringues and rustic sandwiches. Book ahead, as the place gets busy at weekends, and if you can, ask to sit near the front of the café to avoid the bustle of the open kitchen at the back. Without a booking, you can pop in for freshly baked sweets, from a morsel of marshmallow to a wedding-worthy layer cake.

—

44 Theobald's Road, WC1X 8NW.

020 7242 8330

www.beasofbloomsbury.com

Chancery Lane or Holborn tube.

BRANCHES: Farringdon EC1M 6BY; St Paul's EC4M 9BX.

✷ SAVOY

The stunning experience (and rather hefty bill) means afternoon tea at the Savoy is for most a once-in-a-lifetime treat. But it's the Savoy, the most famous hotel in the world, a self-contained belle epoque world of limitless luxury: of course it's going to be breathtaking. Tea is served in the Thames Foyer, which following the hotel's £220 million refurb (really) is a pillared and chandeliered fantasy of gold and contentment. In a central birdcage-like structure, a pianist provides lustrous American jazz (with the odd cheeky pop cover woven in); the menu is fairly traditional, with finger sandwiches (cucumber and mint, Scottish salmon, Wiltshire ham), bijou cakes, pastries and fluffy scones. It probably doesn't need to be pointed out that champagne is a speciality here, and practically compulsory.

—

100 Strand, WC2R 0EW.

020 7420 2111

www.fairmont.com

Charing Cross or Covent Garden tube.

✷ CORINTHIA HOTEL

The Corinthia may not have the decades of tradition that many other London five-stars flaunt so proudly, but it's no less indulgent, flawlessly serving tradition in a contemporary environment. With what must be one of the capital's most grand and sparkly chandeliers at its centre, the bustling lobby lounge is where it all happens – or if the sun's shining you can sit in the peaceful courtyard. The list of refreshments is extensive and includes Ceylon Orange Pekoe and 1885 Afternoon Blend, all served in gilt-edged china; helpfully, a 'tea sommelier' is on hand to help pick your tea, so to speak. Cakes are 'seasonally inspired', which means that as well as flawless scones, you might see plum amaretto tart, or orange blossom choux with macerated kumquat. Spoilt for choice? Leftovers can be discreetly packaged to take away.

—

Whitehall Place, SW1A 2BD.
020 7321 3150
www.corinthia.com
Embankment tube.

✵ BROWN'S

This ultra-luxurious hotel situated in the swankiest location on the Monopoly board offers unfettered indulgence from the moment you step past the be-hatted doormen and marble pillars of the entrance. Despite dating to 1837, Brown's is not suspended in time: in The English Tea Room, antique furniture is stylishly counterpointed by modern art, while the menu runs the gamut from traditional to playful. Its changing themed afternoon teas have ranged from a murder mystery special (in honour of Agatha Christie, once a regular guest) to one with a Christmas twist (complete with a carol-playing pianist). Whether classic or unusual, the cake stand delivers a sophisticated assortment of sandwiches, golden lacquered scones and intricate pâtisserie, plus slices of cake served from a trolley, complemented by 17 teas from the Brown's leaf library.

—

33 Albermarle Street, W1S 4BP.
020 7518 4155
www.roccofortehotels.com
Green Park tube.

✵ FORTNUM & MASON

Official grocer to the royal household, and with a history of flogging fancy foodstuffs stretching all the way back to 1707, Fortnum & Mason knows how to lay on a decent spread. Take the wood-panelled elevator up to the department store's fourth floor where the doors open out on to the Diamond Jubilee Tea Salon with its crisp white linen tablecloths, eau de nil china and tinky-tonky piano music. Immaculately turned-out staff go to and fro with cake stands full of cucumber sandwiches, scones and exquisitely executed pâtisserie. They also visit each table with the 'cake carriage' – a heavenly tray packed with tarts, cakes, éclairs and fancies – while specialist 'tearistas' will talk you through some 150 single-estate teas and blends from across the globe. Unsurprisingly, booking ahead is advised.

—

181 Piccadilly, W1A 1ER.
020 7734 8040
www.fortnumandmason.com
Piccadilly Circus or Green Park tube.

✷ THE LANESBOROUGH

Having undergone an elaborate, two-and-a-half-year refurbishment – which didn't overlook a single gilded cushion, marble pillar or filigreed panel – this London institution stands proud beside the tourist nexus of Hyde Park Corner and Knightsbridge. There are few hotel entrances as grand as that of The Lanesborough, from the top-hatted doormen to the Regency stylings of the lobby leading to the Céleste, the glass-roofed restaurant, which is bedecked in sky blue and gold with cornicing and chandeliers the size of tractor tyres. The afternoon tea menu features gluten- and dairy-free options (these need to be booked in advance), as well as the 'prestige', which for a little extra money gets you truffle on your egg sandwich, caviar on your salmon and a glass of champagne alongside your tea.

—

Hyde Park Corner, SW1X 7TA.
020 7259 5599
www.lanesborough.com
Hyde Park Corner tube.

✷ CLARIDGE'S

This grande dame of London's luxury hotel scene is well practised in the finer details. Afternoon tea takes place in the serene, art deco surrounds of the bloom-filled Foyer, whose thick-pile carpets and high ceiling absorb any noise (apart from the pleasant piano). The goodies arrive beautifully presented on a silver stand (exquisite sandwiches, fresh scones, and, of course, fanciful pastries such as a picture-perfect éclair filled with strawberry-and-peach crème pâtissière), while discreet staff are always one step ahead of your needs. There's even a kids' afternoon tea, with dainty fairy cakes and a menu which doubles up as a colouring book. The seamless set-up has been honed during Claridge's 150-year reign, which is just as well given the eye-watering (though justified) price.

—

49 Brook Street, W1K 4HR.
020 7629 8860
www.claridges.co.uk
Bond Street tube.

✷ THE GORING

It's no wonder this historic hotel, a rock-cake's-throw from Buck Palace, has the royal seal of approval: the whole place makes you feel like a monarch even if you've just stepped off the 73 bus from Stoke Newington. The Goring is less flashy than some of its five-star cousins across the city, making afternoon tea here a calming and pleasantly old-fashioned experience. It is taken either in the sunshine-yellow conservatory, with its grand oil paintings and sky-high windows overlooking the veranda, or the cosy adjoining lounge. There's nothing on the menu to offend the conservative – cucumber sandwiches, scones, pastries – but it's all impeccably done, and the tea list offers everything from lapsang souchong to a fragrant rosebud infusion. Bubbles come in the form of Bollinger: if it's good enough for the Windsors, it's good enough for us.

Beeston Place, SW1W 0JW.
020 7396 9000
www.thegoring.com
Victoria tube.

MAKE SURE THAT YOU GET YOUR SLICE
OF THE CUCUMBER
BEHIND YOU THERE IS NOTHING
POTATO
FELL DOWN
FEAR OF ILLUSTRATIONS
COME OUT OF YOUR HOLE
I DONT HAVE A HEAD BUT STILL I MUST GO TO WORK
THOUGHTS
DON'T TOUCH IT
HOMEMADE IS BEST
FREEDOM
THANK YOU FOR THE SWORD
I LIKE IT VERY MUCH

✷ SKETCH

It's rare to find a restaurant where the toilets are more famous than the food, but this Mayfair venue has plenty to offer besides its futuristic all-white, egg-shaped cubicles in which an ambient nature soundtrack plays. The tea itself is thoroughly good fun. All the classic elements have been given a Sketch twist: the bone china is decorated with playful illustrations by David Shrigley; a finger sandwich comes topped with caviar and a perfect disc of quail egg; and Converse-sporting staff are dressed in utilitarian ensembles designed by Richard Nicoll. It's all terribly cool. The icing on the cake? It's the Gallery dining space with its plush pink booths and a domed ceiling which will make you feel like you're dining inside a giant fondant fancy.

—

9 Conduit Street, W1S 2XG.
020 7659 4500
www.sketch.london
Oxford Circus tube.

✷ BAKE-A-BOO

This unashamedly pink and chintzy tea room is a place of pilgrimage for those who love cakes but can't stomach gluten, dairy, eggs or sugar. It has an extensive selection of bakes so good you won't notice they're lacking a few traditional (apparently non-essential) ingredients. Highlights of the afternoon tea include vegan scones with coconut cream and perfectly crumbly shortbread. There may be more luxurious afternoon teas in London for the non-allergic (see The Lanesborough on p119), but at under £20 per person this is not cynical pricing. Mismatched vintage china and an abundance of bunting make it a popular destination for hen parties and baby showers, though be warned it's only open from Friday to Sunday, and advance bookings are required for afternoon tea, for which there are two sittings at 1pm and 4pm.

—

86 Mill Lane, NW6 1NL.
020 7435 1666
www.bake-a-boo.com
West Hampstead tube.

SEVEN MORE

- **THE ORANGERY**
  The palatial building and regal formal gardens make this a truly elegant afternoon tea, though one best enjoyed during summer.
  Kensington Palace, Kensington Gardens, W8 4PX. High Street Kensington tube.

- **HIGH TEA OF HIGHGATE (pictured)**
  You can build your own afternoon tea at this neighbourhood tearoom, with scones, a slice of cake and a proper pot of tea.
  50 Highgate High Sreet, N6 5HX. Highgate tube.

- **IVY CHELSEA GARDEN**
  Fancy but affordable afternoon tea served in a pretty garden terrace – the perfect spot for champagne and cakes.
  197 King's Road, SW3 5EQ. Sloane Square tube.

- **BETTY BLYTHE**
  This dinky tearoom serves its treats on pretty vintage crockery and encourages themed dress-ups for hen dos and parties.
  73 Blythe Road, W14 0HP. Kensington Olympia Overground.

- **THE DORCHESTER**
  One of the best hotel afternoon teas in London – elegant, intimate, traditional, but without a hint of stuffy service.
  Park Lane, W1K 1QA. Hyde Park Corner tube.

- **ORANGE PEKOE**
  Loose-leaf tea is the star here, though the laid-back afternoon tea is just as enjoyable. Plus it's an excuse to explore brilliant Barnes.
  3 White Hart Lane, SW13 0PX. Barnes Bridge rail.

- **THE RITZ**
  Book well in advance for this tourist honey-trap. It's glitzy and grand and full of people enjoying a special occasion.
  150 Piccadilly, W1J 9BR. Green Park tube.

After a morning spent in the edifying surrounds of a cultural institute - or satisfyingly spending cash - there's nothing like a refreshing cup of tea and slice of cake. Luckily, some of London's best museums, galleries and shops double up as some of the best cafés in town.

CULTURE, SHOP, TEA BREAK

RAGING BULL
EASY St
THE ROAD TO RUIN

THE PROUD ARCHIVIST

Occupying a prime corner on the so-called 'Haggerston Riviera', this spacious canalside spot does many things right. It has plenty of tables overlooking the water with the narrowboats surfing by, making it a great place to pause for brunch and lunch. It offers down-to-earth food (French toast; bacon buttie; soups; sandwiches) that's well-priced. And there's also a good bar with guest ales, wines and cocktails, meaning once you've taken part in The Proud Archivist's more cerebral pursuits, you can enjoy rewards of another kind. The gallery exhibits well-chosen contemporary work from local and international artists, and there's also an array of events and activities including live music, comedy, yoga, lectures and film screenings. If you're planning to café hop, the wonderful Towpath is just a few minutes away (see p166).

—

2-10 Hertford Road, N1 5ET.
020 3598 2626
www.theproudarchivist.co.uk
Haggerston Overground.

Fresh
Orange
Juice

SOMERSET HOUSE

There are an overwhelming number of cafés to choose from at the Thameside culture hub Somerset House. Skye Gyngell – the chef who turned a garden-centre café (see p163) into a Michelin-starred destination – wowed when she opened the wallet-raiding Spring restaurant here in 2014. But she also offers a taste of Spring on a tighter budget in her conservatory-style Salon, where a concise menu and garden-inspired cocktails are perfect for a light lunch or apéritif. A more butch take on the seasons (plus riverside views) can be had at Tom's Terrace, which serves masterful renditions of comfort food favourites on the waterfront. Somerset House also finds space for Tom's Deli (good for a brief coffee break), and Tom's Kitchen, which comes without the views but a solid menu (branches also at Chelsea, St Katharine Docks and Canary Wharf). The latest addition is Pennethorne's – a sophisticated café-bar serving everything from breakfast to dinner. And most informal is a handy Fernandez & Wells (see p45), which features café breakfasts and lunch and the option of tea outside in the striking Palladian courtyard.

—

Strand, WC2R 1LA.
Spring Salon: 020 3011 0115, www.springrestaurant.co.uk
Tom's Kitchen: 0207 845 4646, www.tomskitchen.co.uk
Fernandez & Wells: 0207 420 9408,
www.fernandezandwells.com
Temple tube.

✷ KENWOOD HOUSE

The food at this English Heritage stately home is somewhat outshone by its surroundings: the eighteenth-century abode itself, remodelled by the architect Robert Adam, is stunning, as are the landscaped gardens. The house's history is of passing interest (the last resident was brewing tycoon Edward Guinness), and the art collection is amazing, featuring works by Rembrandt and Turner. The Brew House Café is canteen-style but bright and bustling, with generously filled sandwiches, good cakes (try the banana muffins) and cooked breakfast or soup on the hot plates, while the smaller Steward's Room serves more health-conscious fare. Look out for events celebrating seasonal produce ('Rhubarb Festival' is fun). If weather permits, eat outside on the very pleasant terrace. Expect to walk across the Heath for 25 minutes from Whitestone Walk to reach it (although there's also a car park just two minutes away).

—

Hampstead Lane, NW3 7JR.
020 8348 1286
www.english-heritage.org.uk
Hampstead or Golders Green tube.

✻ THE NATIONAL CAFÉ BY PEYTON & BYRNE

With London restaurant fashion so hung up on exposed brick, bare concrete and unfinished wood, the National Café's twee wainscotting and tinkly tearoom vibe is refreshing, and a haven from the selfie-stick insanity of Trafalgar Square outside. The food is a bit more modern, though: from the baked eggs with kale and chilli at breakfast through gastropub-type lunches and dinners, it's all a good representation of British cooking (although in the way of the P&B chain, mildly uncomfortably pricey). Next to the bistro is a more informal self-service area, with a table heaving under the weight of pastries and cakes. There are packaged sandwiches to pop on a tray and tea in paper cups. It's not the only place Peyton & Byrne serve refreshments to museumgoers – you'll also find the cafés at the Royal Academy of Arts, The Wallace and the Imperial War Museum among others – but this is the most charming.

—

Trafalgar Square, WC2N 4DN.
020 7747 5942
www.peytonandbyrne.co.uk
Charing Cross tube.
BRANCHES: Royal Academy of Arts W1J 0BD; The Wallace Collection W1U 3BN; IWM London SE1 6HZ.

✷ TANGERINE DREAM CAFÉ

The gorgeous Physic Garden in Chelsea's heartland, with its carefully maintained lawns, winding pathways and pretty collections of medicinal plants, is a secret sanctuary for Londoners in search of serenity. It's just as well, as you have to wander through the gardens en route to the café (and pay a £9.90 entrance fee; kids go free). The café itself has a church-hall feel to it, and the trestle table centrepiece heaving with fruit- and vegetable-filled savouries and cakes certainly puts one in mind of a fête, in a very good way. Choose from delicate tarts filled with goats' cheese or sun-dried tomatoes and golden-crusted salmon coulibiac. Then follow with incredibly moist orange-and-almond cake, chunky courgette-and-walnut loaf, or rhubarb-topped cheesecake. The food is clearly inspired by the botanical. There are tables inside, but the best spot, naturally, is outdoors at the awning-covered tables that overlook the gardens.

—

Chelsea Physic Garden, 66 Royal Hospital Road, SW3 4HS.
020 7349 6464
www.tangerinedream.uk.com
Sloane Square tube.

✷ V&A

As befits an institute celebrating the very best in art and design, the museum restaurant at the V&A (the oldest of its kind in the world) is truly gorgeous wherever you choose to sit. The courtyard space, with its ornamental pond, is heavenly on warm days; the Farrow & Ball-esque canteen is also quite chic; and for antique, decorative charm there are the three high-Victorian dining rooms, named Poynter, Morris and Gamble. Each manifests a different aspect of nineteenth-century design theory – Gamble is the best, with sinuous Ionic columns, exquisite enamelled tiles and preachy Evangelical maxims ('hunger is the best sauce') disapproving of your excess through the medium of stained glass. The food is lovely too: cakes mainly, with sandwiches and daily hot lunch specials.

—

Cromwell Road, SW7 2RL.
020 7942 2000
www.vam.ac.uk
South Kensington tube.

LONDON REVIEW CAKE SHOP

Bloomsbury's London Review Bookshop is beautifully curated, well-loved and charming to shop in. So it follows that its adjoining café is as carefully considered. There are lovely homemade cakes – rose and pistachio, chocolate and Guinness, lemon and courgette – as well as a small menu of quiches, sandwiches and salads. Tea is a ritual here, with certain infusions served in beautiful glassware that lets you watch the loose leaves unfurl as they brew. You can cram into the small indoor space, or order to take away and enjoy your cuppa at one of the tables in the rear courtyard. Just remember to buy a book first, of course.

—

14 Bury Place, WC1A 2JL.
020 7269 9045
www.londonreviewbookshop.co.uk
Holborn tube.

London Review Bookshop

✷ ROSE BAKERY

Unless you're a sneaker aficionado, or a student at the London College of Fashion, you might not have come across Dover Street Market, the cutting-edge high fashion emporium created by Comme des Garçons-founder Rei Kawakubo in Mayfair. The sixth-floor bakery is as stylish as the rest of the store: there's earthen crockery, magazines (Dazed & Confused, i-D, Highsnobiety) strewn for casual reading and simple communal sharing tables. The cakes are to savour: the mini carrot cakes fit for one are a delight and a constant, and the rest change with the seasons (chocolate brownies come winter; lemon polenta cake come summer). The food here is also excellent – seasonal, ambitious and exciting – and the Union Roasted coffee is perfectly smooth.

—

17-18 Dover Street, W1S 4LT.
020 7518 0687
www.london.doverstreetmarket.com
Green Park tube.

SEVEN MORE

- **2&4 (pictured)**
  Pop into this antique shop-café for a coffee and a slice of homemade cake, and leave with a vintage sideboard. Oops.
  2-4 Southgate Road, N1 3JW. Haggerston Overground.

- **BOOKS FOR COOKS**
  Cookbook obsessives can spend hours in this tiny, specialist shop – the café tests the cookbooks and serves the results.
  4 Blenheim Crescent, W11 1NN. Ladbroke Grove tube.

- **AIDA**
  A window seat yeilds good Shoreditch-people-watching – safer for your wallet than ogling this boutique's clothes.
  133 Shoreditch High Street, E1 6JE. Old Street tube.

- **CONRAN KITCHEN**
  Imagine your home is as beautiful as the Conran Store by settling among the for-sale furniture in this in-situ café.
  55 Marylebone High Street, W1U 5HS. Regent's Park tube.

- **TATE CAFÉ**
  Table service helps this gallery café feel relaxing despite the bustle. It runs the gamut from a pot of tea to steak and chips.
  1 Bankside, SE1 9TG. Southwark tube.

- **BOND & BROOK**
  Fenwick's in-store offering is far superior to your usual department store café. Refined food that fits the smart crowd.
  63 New Bond Street, W1S 1RQ. Bond Street tube.

- **NO67**
  The South London Gallery is blessed with No67 – locals love it for relaxed and peaceful coffee, cake, lunch and dinner.
  65-67 Peckham Road, SE5 8UH. Peckham Rye Overground.

Play a game of draughts while you enjoy a coffee, stroke a cat as you tuck into your cake, or sip on a bloody Mary as you lounge by a poolside - yes, all in London, and all in these unusual or alfresco cafés.

UNUSUAL & ALFRESCO

UNUSUAL

THE ATTENDANT

Most first-time attendees of the Attendant go along purely for the novelty. And fair enough, it's in a converted men's lavatory. Interestingly though, people keep coming back. Why? Because it's amazing. The coffee (beans sourced from Caravan up the road in King's Cross, milk from a single, handpicked farm down in Somerset) is of the highest quality and served with passion and care. Meals (simple breakfasts, salads, roast-veg sandwiches) are prepared onsite, with ingredients bought the previous evening from New Covent Garden Market. As you might expect, the space itself is extremely wee (there's a second, much larger branch in Shoreditch, which isn't in a former toilet), and, while hardly the priciest place in Fitzrovia, you can expect to spend more than a penny.

—

27a Foley Street, W1W 6DY.
020 7637 3794
www.the-attendant.com
Goodge Street tube.
BRANCHES: Shoreditch EC2A 3JL.

✳ LOOK MUM NO HANDS!

London's not short of cycle cafés, from Broadway Market's Lock 7 and Spitalfields' Peloton & Co to Soho's Rapha Cycle Club, but you don't have to be a die-hard fan of two wheels to enjoy this Clerkenwell offering. Okay, so there are bikes in the windows, parts hanging from the ceiling and it does screen the Tour de France in summer, but the crowd is often more Macbook Pro than pro cyclist. The décor is workshop-chic (white walls, bare bulbs and sanded wooden tables) and the menu ranges from fry-ups to fruit and yoghurt, with everything in between – the toasted banana and walnut bread with cinnamon butter will change your life. LMNH can get pretty busy, so if you're not prepared to wait, try its sister venue on Hackney's Mare Street.

—

49 Old Street, EC1V 9HX.

020 7253 1025

www.lookmumnohands.com

Old Street tube.

BRANCHES: Hackney, E8 3RH.

✷ CEREAL KILLER CAFÉ

It's quite fashionable to knock Cereal Killer for being overpriced and gimmicky: the nadir of east London hipster balderdash. What's often overlooked is how fun the place is. And who (honestly) doesn't like cereal? Choose from 120 different varieties, including tantalising foreign exotica like 'Applezings', 'Quisp' or 'Frosties Zucaritas', then pick a milk you fancy splashing over it (such as soya, coconut or hazelnut). Better yet, take a chance on the quirky 'cocktails': 'Bran Gran Thank You Ma'am' (bran flakes/granola/raisins/soy milk) or 'Double Rainbow' (Froot Loops/Fruity Pebbles/freeze-dried marshmallows/strawberry milk). The décor is pitch-perfect 1990s kitsch: there's retro videogames and Spice Girls paraphernalia. At the Camden outlet you can even sit on old-school cartoon duvets as you scoff your sweet, sugary bowl of joyfulness.

—

139 Brick Lane, E1 6SB.

020 3601 9100

www.cerealkillercafe.co.uk

Shoreditch High Street Overground.

BRANCHES: Camden NW1 8AH.

✳ LADY DINAH'S CAT EMPORIUM

Shoreditch is a sucker for novelty gimmicks, and this cat-filled café is leader of the pack. Its mauve-fronted, two-floor dining room – with patterned carpets and knowingly twee cake stands – is home to a family of felines, who mainly nap in the cosy beds and padded boxes set out for that purpose. Paying customers (a £6 entry fee goes towards the residents' welfare) are the moggies' guests, so there's no cuddling, no unsolicited advances, no feeding and no flash photography. However, if a cat approaches you, you're welcome to stroke it as you tuck into homespun afternoon teas including scones, moist yellow sponge cakes and chunky red-velvet cupcakes with thick splodges of cream-cheese frosting. Advance booking is required for afternoon tea; at other times, turn up on spec for a 'moggiato' (of course).

—

152-154 Bethnal Green Road, E2 6DG.
020 7729 0953
www.ladydinahs.com
Shoreditch High Street Overground.

✺ FRIZZANTE AT HACKNEY CITY FARM

Priding itself on its association with the 'agriturismo' movement (a term referring to the Italian practice of smallholders welcoming tourists into their home and inviting them to sample their produce), Frizzante makes much of its enviable location within the bounds of Hackney City Farm. Somewhat less pedantic about sourcing than its Mediterranean muses (well, no one wants to see Larry The Lamb slaughtered in front of the kids just so you can be assured of the provenance of your chop), it still does very well with the produce of the farm and nearby garden. Cooking is imaginative and consistent, with strong veggie options for lunch and dinner. Fair warning: at daytimes and weekends it becomes a bit of a crèche, but on summer evenings with the odd bird twittering about the exposed beams you could (just about) believe you're in Tuscany.

—

1a Goldsmith's Row, E2 8QA.
020 7739 2266
www.frizzanteltd.co.uk
Cambridge Heath Overground.

PIGS

✷ DRAUGHTS

The jumbo-sized railway arches by Haggerston station have played host to all manner of hip openings. Noodle meister Tonkotsu East (two doors down) is anything but a flash in the pan, and dining and arts space Trip (by the canal) boasts an eclectic programme of yoga classes, dance workshops and jazz gigs, alongside rotating chefs-in-residence. Draughts fits in. In London's first-ever board game café, patrons are invited to rock up with a small gang of like-minded coves and spend an evening (on weekdays it opens at 5pm) or a lazy weekend afternoon playing one of around 500 board games including Scrabble, Risk, and Monopoly, as well as retro/foreign editions, and, if you prefer, Hungry Hungry Hippos. As you'd expect from the area, the beer is craft and the food (light salads, charcuterie boards) is tasty and trendy.

—

337 Acton Mews, E8 4EA.
No phone.
www.draughtslondon.com
Haggerston Overground.

✷ DRINK SHOP & DO

The name says everything you need to know about this King's Cross café. Drink: coffee, tea, cocktails and more. Shop: gifts, cards, sweets in jars. Do: well, anything from screen printing and clay modelling to building Lego robots in a series of free and cheap craft nights and workshops. With its retro furniture, secondhand china and bright art prints, DS&D has a cutesy vibe, though the space (once a Victorian bathhouse) makes it feel grand and special. Afternoon teas (hen dos and parties book these with a 'craft' element) are available on weekends, or if you're feeling worse for wear on a Sunday, try the 'Bloody Marys and Board Games' session. There's also purely grown-up fun downstairs in Drink Shop & Do's bar and club.

—

9 Caledonian Road, N1 9DX.
020 7278 4335
www.drinkshopdo.com
King's Cross tube.

THE WREN

Since setting up in the previously disused St Nicholas Cole Abbey, the folks behind The Wren (favourite of discerning City workers, since it's only open weekdays) have done blissfully little to alter the space: marble floors, soaring stained glass windows and pulpit all remain. The church is something of a patchwork, since the original medieval building was destroyed in the Great Fire, rebuilt by Christopher Wren, bombed during the Blitz and reconstructed in the 1960s. As for what's on offer now, the coffee (made with Workshop Coffee Co beans) is superb, the sandwiches and cakes are fabulous (the carrot cake and banana bread can sell out within the hour) and the excellent pastries come from Sally Clarke's in Notting Hill.

—

114 Queen Victoria Street, EC4V 4BJ.
No phone.
www.thewrencoffee.com
Mansion House tube.

*PORRIDGE w/ CREAM + GOLDEN SYRUP £3.50
*CROISSANT w/ JAM £2.50
LUNCH TODAY
SANDWICH
GOATS CHEESE, HONEY & THYME
TOASTIE
TALEGGIO & ROSEMARY & FIG
ON TOAST
MANCHEGO & HONEY
(2 SLICES)
UPHOLSTERERS
THREE PIECE SUITES
RE-COVERED
703 2686

FOWLDS

Housed in the dinky former cutting room of a still-operational upholsterers, this community-run café – a lovely find just off the Kennington-to-Camberwell drag – was funded and established by residents. When not baking goods for the enterprise (such as lavishly iced carrot cake with walnut-studded sponge), they can be found sipping Square Mile coffee and cold-pressed juices on the close-set benches of the charming, unreconstructed interior, or quaffing prosecco on the makeshift terrace in the warmer months. Breakfasts range from an abstemious half-grapefruit to porridge topped with a decadent duo of cream and golden syrup, plus modish options such as granola with orange, star anise, roasted plums and yoghurt; for lunch, there's a trio of sandwiches with changing fillings. And the trump card? It's just yards from leafy Burgess Park.

—

3 Addington Square, SE5 7JZ.
020 3417 4500
www.facebook.com/fowldscafe
Oval tube.

✷ BEN'S HOUSE

This city is packed with individuals, and Ben Leask, the jovial personality behind this charming shop-café, is not only one of the capital's many one-offs, he also stocks the produce of London's many unique businesses. In this simple, modern shop, you can pick up artisan ingredients you never knew were 'cured, curated and crafted in London', from Château Tooting wine and Kernel Brewery beer to charcuterie by The Gay Farmer and even a London version of dulce de leche. Nab one of the tables dotted around the shop, or retire to the stylish snug and enjoy a Volcano coffee (roasted in Peckham) with, say, a savoury deep-filled quiche, a Ginger Pig sausage roll, or a devilishly sweet banana-and-salted-caramel Crosstown doughnut. It's a proper taste of London.

—

64 Grafton Way, W1T 5DP.
020 7388 0850
www.benshouse.london
Warren Street tube.

CARLTON
HOUSE
Ben's
HOUSE
CURED CREATED CRAFTED
in London

✷ TRIO

This large, bright café has nailed a tricky balancing act: it's a carefully thought through child-friendly destination that considers parents equally. The close attention to detail is evident: from the ample buggy space and toys that span age groups to the diverting mobile in the well-appointed changing facilities. While the adults enjoy a cup of joe courtesy of Mission Coffee Works with a fortifying cake from the tempting spread, or scarf a truly delicious gourmet toastie with a homemade juice, their kids can go nuts in the designated play area, or attend workshops ranging from dance classes to mask-making. Staff are angels, making zero fuss about mess, noise or pint-sized explorers, and the children's menu is just right. If you don't have little ones, try Anderson & Co over the road.

—

182 Bellenden Road, SE15 4BW.
0207 635 4175
www.triobellendenroad.co.uk
Peckham Rye Overground.

PAPER & CUP

As if the reasonably priced Union Coffee, delicious brownies and pleasing distance from the perenially cool Shoreditch High Street wasn't enough, Paper & Cup is also a not-for-profit social enterprise, providing training and work for vulnerable people with the support of Spitalfields Crypt Trust. The shop's white walls, pale wood floors and almost entirely glass front make it feel spacious and light, while the shelves of secondhand books and select records on the wall (Dire Straits, Salt-N-Pepa) not only give you something to browse, buy or borrow, but they also give the place a real sense of character. Grab a table outside for a lovely view of St Leonard's church across the street.

—

18 Calvert Avenue, E2 7JP.

020 7739 5358

www.paperandcup.co.uk

Shoreditch High Street Overground.

BRANCHES: Poplar E3 4AJ.

✳ SCOOTER CAFFE

Time stands still in this one-of-a-kind little place. If it weren't for the wifi, it might feel like you'd travelled back in time to some non-specific decade of the middle of last century: the creaky furniture and vintage coffee machine do their best to convince visitors they've stepped off the streets of Waterloo and into another era. Food is limited to baked-on-the-premises cakes (all wonderful) and a cat roams around settling on any laps she favours. In the best sense, Scooter doesn't belong in London; it's closer to the Paris or Berlin of literary imagination in that it's a proper café-bar, where jazz plays and a strong Campari-based pick-me-up goes down as well as a caffeine-based one. Many patrons tap away at laptops but a paperback seems more appropriate.

—

132 Lower Marsh, SE1 7AE.

020 7620 1421

No website.

Waterloo tube.

CAKEHOLE CAFÉ

Tucked into the back of a vintage homeware shop, this cosy Hoxton tea room has the vibe of a carefully curated jumble sale, with assorted pots, mirrors and tapestries lining its walls. You might struggle to get a seat on a Sunday, when the crowds seek refuge from Columbia Road Flower Market outside, but retro rummagers will be right at home waiting for a table among the cut glass and crockery for sale in the front. Putting the cake in Cakehole is Louise, who runs the café and bakes many of the sweet treats herself – don't miss the coffee and walnut, or the tangy lemon drizzle. There's also a small selection of sandwiches and a cream tea. Open weekends only.

—

Vintage Heaven, 82 Columbia Road, E2 7QB.
No phone.
www.cakeholecafe.co.uk
Hoxton Overground.

THE LIDO CAFÉ

There's a summery feel all year round at this pared-back shabby-chic cantina, with its paper pom-poms, bunting-strewn interior and plum views of the gorgeous art deco Brockwell Lido. You don't have to brave the chilly waters to enjoy the café – it's a popular local haunt even for non-swimmers, especially those with kids. Luxurious breakfasts and brunches can be lingered over with a glass of prosecco or a bloody Mary; the gigantic house burger comes with crisp chips and a superb homemade buttermilk slaw; desserts range from elegant pistachio and cardamom tart to homemade salted-caramel ice-cream sliders; and they all show the skill and scope of the kitchen team. Poolside sundowner cocktails are also a hot ticket – it's like South Beach in south London.

—

Brockwell Lido, Dulwich Road, SE24 0PA.
020 7737 8183
www.thelidocafe.co.uk
Herne Hill rail.

✷ PETERSHAM NURSERIES TEAHOUSE

Petersham Nurseries' Michelin-starred restaurant has had quite the roster of chefs to its name: Skye Gyngell, Greg Malouf and now Damian Clisby, former head chef at Hix Soho. And though the neighbouring Teahouse is more humble, it's still quite unlike any other venue in London: it's a large greenhouse draped in plants, with an uneven sandy floor and mismatched and occasionally rusty furniture. The menu features an informal range of salads, quiches and pastas, with a focus on local produce and garden freshness (think courgettes with ricotta and artichokes), and the cakes are hearty and delicious – plenty of fresh fruit and unusual grain blends, no buttercream. The pricing is slightly ambitious at times, befitting the verdant wonderland of the surroundings, but the atmosphere is jolly and kids can roam freely between table legs.

—

Church Lane, TW10 7AB.
020 8940 5230
www.petershamnurseries.com
Richmond tube.

PAVILION

✵ PAVILION

Like your brunch with a view? Bag a window seat at this café in east London's prettiest park – or better yet, a table outside on the terrace for a prime vista of the lovely lake, complete with fountain and fowl. Inside, light streams in through the little pavilion's glass-domed roof and it's a pleasant place to relax come rain or shine. Coffee is from the nearby Square Mile, meat comes courtesy of high-class butchers Ginger Pig and fresh pastries are piled high on the counter. As well as the usual brunches and posh sandwiches, the menu sometimes features quirkier offerings – fancy a Sri Lankan breakfast, complete with egg curry? Work off the calories afterwards with a turn around the lake on a pedalo, which you can pick up next door.

—

Victoria Park, E9 7DE.
020 8980 0030
www.pavilionlondon.tumblr.com
Bethnal Green or Mile End tube.

✷ TOWPATH

When Towpath opened in 2010 it was a convincingly rustic piece of rus-in-urbe minutes from Kingsland Road. A few more apartment blocks have sprung up around it since then, but it's still a pleasingly pastoral place to sit with a coffee (or tumbler of wine). When it's packed (as it often is), or the weather is less than clement, inside seating is available. The café is idiosyncratically spread over four shallow units with mismatched furniture, and it's easy to wile away the hours watching the buggies, bikes and emboldened birds vie for supremacy on the narrow canal path. The food is homely fare elevated by chefs who really care: expect the best ingredients and lots of passion. Just beware the understandably eccentric opening hours: 9am-dusk, closed Mondays, and also closed Tuesday and Wednesday through deepest winter. Makes sense.

—

36 De Beauvoir Crescent, N1 5SB.
No phone.
No website.
Haggerston Overground.

SEVEN MORE

- **BONNINGTON CAFÉ**
  A right-on community space that's been around since the 1980s. Brace for hearty, cheap, world food by rotating member cooks.
  11 Vauxhall Grove, SW8 1TD. Vauxhall tube.

- **FARM:SHOP**
  Ingredients are grown in the shop (using polytunnels, an indoor allotment and lots of tech!) and then served in the café.
  20 Dalston Lane, E8 3AZ. Dalston Junction Overground.

- **BISCUITEERS (pictured)**
  Ice your own biscuits or buy pre-made – there are animals, cartoon characters and seasonally themed biccies to crunch on.
  Two branches, including 194 Kensington Park Road, W11 2ES. Ladbroke Grove tube.

- **ZIFERBLAT**
  Tea, food and wifi are all free in this alt-café – you only need pay for your time. It's 6p per minute capped at five hours.
  388 Old Street, EC1V 9LT. Shoreditch High Street Overground.

- **THE GARDEN CAFÉ**
  Run by chain Benugo, this simple café is all about the location: off Oxford Street on an elevated, historic, oasis-like garden.
  Brown Hart Gardens, Duke Street, W1K 6TD. Bond Street tube.

- **THE REGENT'S BAR & KITCHEN**
  Situated in the tranquil Regent's Park, this café is a dream come summer, with barbecues, stone-baked pizza and ice cream.
  Inner Circle, Regent's Park, NW1 4NU. Baker Street tube.

- **LAUDERDALE HOUSE**
  Lots of picnic tables set in the picturesque Waterlow Park make this humble café a must-visit.
  Waterlow Park, Highgate Hill, N6 5HG. Highgate tube.

Stanmore
Golders Green
Highgate
132
Crouch E
A1
Harrow
Neasden
A406
Wembley
Hampstead
Cricklewood
124
28
A41
99
Kentish Town
73
Camden Town
Willesden
Kensal Green
Kilburn
Perivale
St John's Wood
Maida Vale
A40
11
53
Marylebone
48
42
Notting Hill
109
Acton
Ealing
119
Shepherds Bush
Westminst
136
86
121
Hammersmith
100
135
Chiswick
A4
Sloane Square
Brentford
Vauxh
Barnes
Fulham
Battersea
Kew
Putney
Wandsworth
A205
Clapham
54
A3
Richmond
163

Upper Clapton
A12
Leytonstone
Ilford
Leyton
21
Stoke Newington
46
54
108
Lower Clapton
ghbury
14
Forest Gate
Canonbury
A10
102
23
97
Hackney
Stratford
West Ham
Islington
34
East Ham
Bow
16
Shoreditch
Plaistow
Barbican
Stepney
verpool Street
Limehouse
Poplar
Rotherhithe
Waterloo
London Bridge
Bermondsey
95
90
160
Isle of Dogs
A102
Woolwich
69
Charlton
66
Deptford
Greenwich
Oval
155
55
33
Welling
A202
Camberwell
41
Blackheath
Peckham
59
36
Lewisham
A2
158
Brixton
162
Chislehurst

SEE PAGE 170

CAMDEN TOWN
32
Angel
151
Euston Square
12
Warren Street
Great Portland Street
Regent's Park
156
Russell Square
CLERKENWELL
88
FITZROVIA
114
Theobalds Rd
82
Goodge Street
74
144
110
138
56
15
Chancery Lane
Holborn
Tottenham Court Road
43
98
80
Oxford Circus
Bond Street
78
Fleet St
Covent Garden
72
45
120
123
93
39
89
87
MAYFAIR
Leicester Square
Temple
131
117
Piccadilly Circus
115
134
140
118
Charing Cross
Embankment
Green Park
ST. JAMES'S
116
94

SOUTH HACKNEY
166
129
150
Pownall Rd
24
70
62
Victoria Park Rd
New N Rd
Laburnum St
25
38
165
104
HAGGERSTON
148
107
161
BETHNAL GREEN
Bethnal Green
71
159
20
27
147
Great Easten St
Old St
79
35
146
145
Barbican
BARBICAN
Liverpool Street
19
Cavell St
STEPNEY
Aldgate East
St Paul's
Aldgate
WHITECHAPEL
Mansion House
Monument
Tower Hill
77
London Bridge
WAPPING

INDEX

EAST

SOUTH CENTRAL: VAUXHALL, WATERLOO, LONDON BRIDGE & BERMONDSEY

SOUTH & SOUTH-WEST

WEST CENTRAL: BELGRAVIA, KNIGHTSBRIDGE, KENSINGTON, NOTTING HILL & LADBROKE GROVE

WEST

Italics indicate branches.

Frances Lincoln Limited
A subsidiary of Quarto Publishing Group UK
74–77 White Lion Street
London N1 9PF

Café London

Design: Sarah Allberrey

A catalogue record for this book is available from the British Library.

ISBN 978-0-7112-3745-2

Printed and bound in China

9 8 7 6 5 4 3 2 1

Front cover: Hej.
Back cover: Bea's of Bloomsbury (top), Prufrock (bottom right) and Counter Café (bottom left).
Opening page: Snaps + Rye.
p2 Prufrock; p3 Rochelle's Canteen; p4 Esters; p7 Fernandez & Wells; p8 Trade.
Opposite: The Spoke.